BRITAIN AND EUROPE

JEREMY BLACK

Britain and Europe

A Short History

HURST & COMPANY, LONDON

First published in the United Kingdom in 2019 by
C. Hurst & Co. (Publishers) Ltd.,
41 Great Russell Street, London, WC1B 3PL
© Jeremy Black, 2019
All rights reserved.
Printed in Scotland by Bell & Bain Ltd, Glasgow

The right of Jeremy Black to be identified as the author of
this publication is asserted by him in accordance with the
Copyright, Designs and Patents Act, 1988.

A Cataloguing-in-Publication data record for this book
is available from the British Library.

ISBN: 9781787381186

This book is printed using paper from registered sustainable
and managed sources.

www.hurstpublishers.com

For Simon Green

CONTENTS

PREFACE

The mastodons on both sides roar with reference to Britain's past with Europe. On 30 May 2018, Lord Malloch-Brown, a former Foreign Office minister, told BBC Radio Four listeners that Britain should not leave the European Union because Europe's problems had a 'horrible habit of infecting us anyway. Appeasement in the 1930s—you name it. For centuries Britain has ignored events on continental Europe at its peril.' Let us leave aside the point that Appeasement represented an engagement with Continental power politics, however misconceived, rather than an abandonment of it. It is another word for cautious restraint, as in Britain's 'appeasement' of Putin's Russia over Georgia and Ukraine, and earlier of Stalin's Soviet Union. Nevertheless, Malloch-Brown made the reasonable point that Britain's history has, at least in part, to be understood in a European context. Here, I will try to provide this context.

Shaping the past in the light of present-day concerns is an integral part of considering and writing history. And so obviously it might appear in a book on Britain and Europe written in the hot, dry and troubled summer of 2018. In part, my new book is an attempt to update my thoughts on the topic, and within a context affected by the excellent work of many others. There is repetition of earlier material where relevant, but, throughout, this is a new book, one with new concerns. Particular attention focuses on a number of questions. Firstly, how similar or dissimilar was Britain to other European countries, and in what respects? Secondly, how far can similarity and difference be understood in terms of convergence, divergence, or roughly parallel tracks? Thirdly, did British people feel themselves to be Europeans, taking an informed and sympathetic interest in what was happening on the Continent, or did their ignorance of Europe lead to insularity and xenophobia? And, fourthly, to what extent was Britain involved in the affairs of the Continent?

Employing the terms Britain and the Continent as building blocks begs a host of questions, including the question of whether it prejudges the topic by ensuring that it is considered in terms of a necessary duality. An alternative conceptualisation puts Europe to the fore, and treats British developments as aspects of a more varied pattern of diversity. That is certainly the case, but should not preclude attention to England, later Britain, as a state that had agency as well as difference. Moreover, this argument can be pushed to suggest that Britain (or part of it) had more in common with the rest of north-west Europe (or part of it) than did the latter with the remainder of Europe.

There are also the contrasts, even tensions, created by overlaps. It might be possible to feel a cultural affinity with aspects of the Continent but, at the same time, a religious or political alienation. Indeed, there is a wealth of conceptual and methodological caveats that can be pushed to the fore. It is better to remain mindful of them while turning to the past. Some of these issues will be addressed in the historical sections, but others will be considered in the last chapter.

The identity of the 'national interest' has been a vexed political topic. In his dedication to Frederick, Prince of Wales of his 1725–31 translation of Paul de Rapin-Thoyras's history of England, originally published in 1723–5, Nicholas Tindal, an Anglican clergyman, declared: 'Your Royal Highness will here perceive, that foreign acquisitions and conquests were generally fatal to England; all increase of empire burdensome to her, except that of the Ocean, which can never be too extensive, as it enlarges and protects her trade, the principal fountain of her riches and grandeur.' That, however, like most texts, had particular meanings, in this case being a warning about rule by the Hanoverian dynasty turning into a policy of Continental expansion.

The 'national interest' was problematic then and is very much so again at present. To help debate the matter, it is helpful to look at the underlying continuities in relations with the Continent. There has always been an interplay between engagement with the Continent and caution about the links; as well as between, on the one hand, ideological views on policy and, on the other, more instrumental concerns. The 'national interest' is often pushed to the fore as an answer or employed in the debate, but in practice is a significant instance of the interplay between the instrumental and the ideological or emotional. While the 'national interest' is linked to the idea of policy as inherently prudential, at the same time, in reality, it is not a given, but, instead, a political construct and one that draws on cultural themes and understandings. Far from there being any simple, causal relationship between the ideological and the instrumental, the structural and the ephemeral, there are other dimensions to policy, including the role of geopolitical concerns, irrespective of the ideology and pressing politics of the moment. In turn, the ideology and politics affect the understanding both of these dimensions and of the need to act.

I have benefited greatly from the comments of Steve Bodger, Bill Gibson, Stephen Rathbone, Nigel Saul and Doug Stokes on an earlier version of this text. Sections were tried out in papers given in Canberra, Exeter, London, New York, Oxford, Paris, Philadelphia and Wilmington. It is a great pleasure to dedicate this book to Simon Green, a much-admired fellow historian and very pleasant as well as thoughtful friend.

FROM THE IRON AGE TO THE REFORMATION

The links between Britain and the Continent are not recent; nor is their deployment for political ends. In 2013, David Cameron, in what was presented as an important speech about Britain's position in Europe, referred to 'Caesar's legions', who had invaded England in 55 and 54 BCE, in arguing that 'We have helped to write European history, and Europe has helped write ours'. Possibly an invasion was not the best example to cite. The spread of Christianity under Roman rule might have been more pertinent, but then Cameron is not an ex-Prime Minister for nothing.

Most of Britain's history, including that of its relations with the Continent, is covered in this chapter, and it would be mistaken, but understandable given the current focus on Brexit, to rush through the period. It is all too easy to treat the pre-industrial, pre-democratic world as of scant relevance to the present situation, as, indeed, 'historic' in the sense that it is past. That view, one strengthened by our being well into a new millennium as well as a new century, would be a reflection of much present-day opinion.

Nevertheless, it is an approach that understates the role of 'deep history', long-standing characteristics that carry forward the impact of past circumstances and that set the parameters within which the events of the present tend to occur and be perceived. Cultural and political trajectories are the product of many years, and not a couple of decades. Much of the pattern of modern Britain was set in the period covered by this chapter, including Christianity, the common law, parliamentary legislation and the territorial boundaries of England and Scotland. These elements were to be worked on in the centuries that followed, but also had to be worked with. Change, moreover, occurred within contexts that were not always as malleable as politicians hoped, a position that continues to the present. To argue that policy changes disprove the existence of 'deep history' is to misunderstand its character and impact.

Pre-Roman

The inhabitants of the British Isles have always come from the Continent, and the end of the land bridge in about 6500 BCE, as sea levels rose after the Ice Age, did not prevent this process. That movement did not ensure any predictable pattern of developments or, indeed, significant (or any) continuing links, but there were important shared elements and clearly some relationships of consequence. Thus, in the Iron Age (800 BCE—100 CE), there were changes in southern Britain which were similar to those of northern France and the Low Countries. In part, this similarity was due to population movements, but their scale, and the extent to which invasion as opposed to peaceful migration and settlement was involved, are unclear. 'Belgic' culture was associated with the development of proto-towns, the use of coins, and the existence of 'states' with monarchical patterns of government, such as in Essex under the tribe of Trinovantes. Yet, there was also variation within Britain: links between the Continent and southern Britain were more frequent and immediate than with northern Britain. This, indeed, encouraged Julius Caesar's two expeditions: he argued that the invasion of Britain was necessary to ending resistance to Rome's recent conquest of France, a convenient, but wrong, assessment.

The Romans

The Romans were to transform the situation in Britain by introducing a system of politics and government through which events elsewhere in Europe had a continuous direct impact in Britain. Much of Britain was to be a province whose destiny was determined from a distant capital. The successful invasion by the Emperor Claudius, launched in 43 CE with the Emperor soon himself present, rapidly brought southern Britain under Roman control, either directly or through those allies whom the Romans were willing to accept. Prefiguring modern debates, the use of the term 'foreign control' can be regarded as misleading, as a claim to universalism was a feature of Roman imperialism, and citizenship ultimately was not to be restricted to Italians, although Rome's opponents could be forgiven for not appreciating this. Similarly, Roman conquest did not necessarily mean expropriation of property (in the pattern of the later Norman Conquest) and the destruction of local religions. Until Christianity became the state religion, the polytheistic nature of the official Olympian cult encouraged an acceptance of diverse religions as long as they were not associated with hostility to Rome, as the Druids were. The adaptability of oral societies was manifested in religious mutations, most obviously the amalgamation of British and Roman gods and cults, as at Bath.

Yet, at the same time, there was much brutality and expropriation in the conquest. Indeed, on a longer timespan, Britain was to

3

have the experience of conquest and rule, or attempted conquest, from the Continent far more than vice versa. For a long time, moreover, this was a key aspect of the collective memory. Nineteenth-century writers offered novels on past episodes of contested conquest, such as Charles Kingsley's *Hereward the Wake: Last of the English* (1866), a novel that helped turn Hereward into a hero. So also with painters, and with the dramatic Boudicca statue near Parliament, *Boadicea and Her Daughters* by Thomas Thornycroft, erected in 1902. Given the planned German invasion in 1940, Operation Sealion, the threat of invasion is a memory that has for many reached to close to the present. It is one very much kept alive through film and other portrayals.

While the Romans conquered much of Britain, notably England and Wales, uniting it for the first time, they did not conquer all of it, principally highland Scotland. North of Hadrian's Wall, much of Northumberland was only held for a while. Ireland was never conquered. The Romans thus demonstrated a central feature of British history: a lack of uniformity that, in part, reflected a variety of local socio-economic systems stemming from what is, for a country of Britain's size, an extraordinary geological and geomorphological range. At the same time, such systems were given historical force by the role of individuals and groups, and the play of contingency. The lack of uniformity helps make multiple histories possible.

To the south of the frontier zone, the generally peaceful nature of Roman rule encouraged a process of Romanisation, although that was largely a function of élite activity. Trade with the Continent developed greatly under Roman rule and this was linked to the growth of ports, notably London. Outside the lowland towns, which were the centres of authority, consumption, and Roman culture (including, eventually, Christianity), Britain was not as thoroughly Romanised or acculturated as other provinces of the empire, for example France and Spain.

For the bulk of the indigenous population, linguistic assimilation to the Latin of government was limited: Latin and Celtic co-existed, only for both of them to be later displaced by Anglo-Saxon.

The End of Roman Britain

Britain's place within the Roman empire was fully demonstrated in the impact both of struggles for power within the Roman élite and army, and also of attacks from 'barbarian' outsiders. Usurpers based in Britain sought control on the Continent. In addition, the break-up of Roman Britain, after 409, into a number of kingdoms suggests that the internal unity of Roman Britain was superficial in many respects below the level of the aristocratic élite. Moreover, the successor kingdoms competed with each other, as well as with 'barbarian' invaders.

The Anglo-Saxon invasions from the fifth century on represented a major new impulse in Britain's relations with the Continent, although Britain was not distinctive in being invaded and becoming post-Roman. Indeed, Scotland, which was not part of the Roman empire, faced successful invasion from Ireland. Separately, as with the Continent, a period of invasion and migration can be seen in terms of a long continuum in British history characterised by such episodes. Thus, alongside change, there was continuity or, rather, the two were often coterminous. Successful invasions continued until that of William III in 1688, although part of the skill of the national tradition was to have that presented as a liberation from Catholic autocracy.

The Anglo-Saxon invasions were to be important to the subsequent discussion both of English history and of English's relations with the Continent. In practice, an emphasis on continuity is suggested by the degree to which Anglo-Saxon settlers occupied an already managed landscape. This process was further accentuated by the survival of many Romano-Britons as slaves and peasants. DNA work suggests a considerable degree of continuity and intermarriage, as, indeed, in more recent centuries.

Within the former Roman empire, the loss of language, towns and Christianity was unique to Britain. The same did not happen in France, Italy, Spain or North Africa, although in western parts of Britain, beyond the Anglo-Saxon advance, Christianity was maintained as a powerful religious force. Furthermore, Celtic Christianity had links with the Continent, while there is archaeological evidence, in the form of amphorae (jars), of Mediterranean trade with Britain in the fifth century.

It would be misleading, therefore, to see changes in terms of British exceptionalism. In practice, the violent disruption of political structures was common to much of the Western Roman empire, while the plague, as in the 670s, bridged political divides. Rich and ornate goods, many from the Continent, found in seventh-century ship burials, notably Sutton Hoo, and in Kentish cemeteries, testify to continuing and new Continental links.

Anglo-Saxon England

Furthermore, Christianity spread again across England. As a result, there was tension over the authority of Rome as opposed to that of the Irish-based Celtic Church, but, thanks to the support of King Oswy of Northumbria at the Synod of Whitby (664), this authority prevailed. The subsequent reputation of the Synod indicates that current contention about Britain and the Continent is scarcely new. After the Reformation, the Synod was to be seen by some Protestant writers as a defeat for a native tradition of Christianity and a triumph for foreign, i.e. Catholic, influences which helped to pervert primitive purity. To them, it represented the fall of the Church, rather as the Norman Conquest caused that of English liberty. Considered differently,

England could be said to have become an active part of a dynamic cultural world, one that looked to Rome, but was held together by ecclesiastical and religious links rather than, as under the Roman empire, by imperial power with its military rationale.

The spread of Catholic rites and papal authority was a more general process in Western Europe, as was the coalescence of kingdoms, which in England eventually produced, in the eighth century, three major ones: Northumbria in the North, Mercia in the Midlands, and Wessex in the South. In Western Europe, a far greater force was created in the late eighth century, in the shape of the French-based Carolingian empire, but that proved transient, fracturing in the mid-ninth century. This ensured a crucial aspect of British relations with the Continent, namely the divided, even fragmented, nature of the Continent for most of the last one-and-a-half millennia, a situation that contrasted with the larger polities that existed across most of the settled areas of Eurasia. For Britain to be geographically peripheral among a number of sovereign states was very different from being autonomous or independent only twenty miles from a powerful empire, as had been the case prior to the Roman invasion in 43 CE.

Ironically, England/Britain was to be put under great pressure not from the Carolingians, who, instead, projected their power into Italy, Germany and, to a far lesser extent, Spain, but, like much of the Continent including France, from a new wave of 'barbarian' invasions in the shape of the Vikings from Scandinavia. In place of the earlier pattern in which Continental influences were felt most directly in the nearest parts of Britain, especially the lowlands of southern and eastern England, the Viking impact was more comprehensive and direct. Aside from the Norse from Norway making major gains in Ireland and Scotland and attacking Wales, the Vikings, specifically the Danes, overran East Anglia, Yorkshire and Mercia in the 860s and 870s. They were eventually halted by Alfred, king of Wessex, a major turning point which also became a key episode in the later national account of a quasi-providential history.

The 'barbarian' attacks of the fourth century had seen troops moved from one part of the Roman empire to another. No such response was offered to the Vikings, although the interrelationship between Danish operations in Britain and northern France appears to have been well understood. There was no Carolingian assistance, but it has been argued that Wessex drew on Carolingian examples for much of its administrative structure. Conversely, there has been an emphasis on giving due weight to the impact of indigenous advances, ideas and traditions.

As with the rulers of northern Spain against the Moors, and the Ottonian emperors of Germany against the Magyars, the later prestige and position of the house of Wessex owed much to its successful resistance to invaders. In the case of the house of Wessex, there was also its subsequent driving back of the Danes, especially in the 900s–920s, such that a kingdom of the English, essentially covering modern England, was created in the tenth century. In the 910s, the Midlands were brought under control. In 927, Athelstan (r. 924–39), Alfred's grandson, conquered the Viking kingdom of York, although it was seized back after his death and not finally reconquered till 954. Probably as a consequence of the influence of Carolingian ideology, specifically that of a Christian empire, Wessex moved towards a notion of kingship different from that of simply the earlier amalgam of kingdoms. At any rate, an English state was defined that did not require precise ethnic or geographical borders.

Difference has been found in the claim that, thanks to agrarian innovation, England was unusually wealthy in Northwestern Europe in proportion to her size and population. It has also been argued that the monetary economy was particularly developed in eastern England, while England as a whole had a common coinage and national taxation. This is held to reflect a marked degree of administrative sophistication and political coherence.

At the same time, the politically contingent nature of such developments attracts attention. Danish attacks resumed in the late tenth century, and in 1016 Cnut became king of all England. As he also became king of Denmark in 1019 and conquered Norway in the 1020s, England became part of a Scandinavian multiple kingdom, although imperial institutions were not created.

As Danish rule ended in 1042, it can appear as an interlude, a throwback to the late ninth century arising from the fortuitous combination of a late burst of Viking activity and, in the person of Aethelred the Unready, a weak and distant English ruler. Danish control in 1016–42 certainly contrasted with the impact and consequences of Norman invasion and rule: Cnut sought to rule, not as a foreign oppressor, but as a lord of both Danes and non-Danes. He was the king of a number of kingdoms, not a monarch seeking to enlarge one kingdom. Within England, Cnut, as inheritor of the Old English monarchy, acted as a legislator for the whole kingdom, and that at a time when the rulers of France could not do so. Moreover, he did what an English king was supposed to do as head of state, not least in supporting local saint cults, and it is instructive that, unlike William, who had a better claim to the throne, he did not have to face rebellions. That the term 'Danish Conquest' was not used, as 'Norman Conquest' was to be, reflected the extent to which England represented to the Danes civilisation, but to the Normans rather the opposite. The Danish period serves as a reminder of the very different possibilities for Continental links that existed. Being a part of a multiple kingdom did not necessarily entail the situation that subsequently prevailed under the Normans and Angevins.

Like William I (r. 1066–87) subsequently, Cnut was also a major actor on a wider stage. This was a novelty, something outside the tradition of the English kingdoms. Earlier, Anglo-Saxon rulers were well aware of the Continent. Alfred went to Rome twice, while Athelstan was related by the marriages of his sisters to the other rulers of Western Europe. Yet, there were major differences between such links and being part of a larger polity, not least one in which England was not the home kingdom of the monarch. A theme through much of this book is that England was generally part of a multi-polity territorial state. This was true for England of the Danish and Norman state, for England and Wales of the Roman, Angevin and Tudor state, and for the whole of the British Isles from the Stuarts in 1603 onwards, until Irish partition in 1922, with the significant addition of Hanover in 1714–1837.

As so often, trends interacted with contingencies. This was true both when Cnut established power and after his death. The short-lived partition agreements of 1016 and 1035 indicated the highly precarious nature of the English state, although neither agreement lasted. It is also clear that it is mistaken to think too rigidly of 'English' and 'foreign'. Moreover, there were significant economic, religious and cultural links between England and the Continent. Trade between the east coast and the Low Countries and the Rhineland was especially important, with wool exports to the Continent of growing value. There were also important cultural links with the Low Countries and the Rhineland, as well as France. Late Anglo-Saxon England was in no way cut off from the Continent but, instead, was open to external influences, a process greatly facilitated by trade and the role of the Church.

At the same time, it was far from clear in the eleventh century what the political relationship between Britain and the Continent would be. In 1042, the house of Wessex was restored in the person of Edward the Confessor. As with France under the later Carolingians, the central political questions of dynastic monarchies, the calibre of the ruler and the nature of the succession ensured a large degree of unpredictability. Yet, there were distinctive differences. The growth of administrative kingship was what distinguished England from France and Germany. The king's peace, the king's courts, the king's writs, the king's taxes, all of which covered the kingdom as a whole, were not matched by the early Capetians, who succeeded the Carolingians, in France. Although seigneurial feudalism affected the administrative structure of the Anglo-Saxon state after the Conquest, the fact that Henry I (r. 1100–35) and Henry II (r. 1154–89) built their own administrative kingship upon it was fundamental in giving English government a different shape and a contrasting feel from that in France. The roots of political centralism in England are thus more ancient and deeper than elsewhere, although this should not lead to an underplaying of the strength of the regional outlook.

On the other hand, two alternative perspectives can be offered. Any stress on the strength of the administrative structure of the Anglo-Saxon state appears less convincing in the case of northern England. Secondly, in England as elsewhere, power in the localities tended to rest with individuals over whom the power of the 'central state' was limited. There was also, at every level, the shared impact of political contingencies. Conversely, this is true for all states, while administrative consistency and political strength always vary within states.

The Norman Conquest

Contingencies came to the fore in 1066 with conquest by William, Duke of Normandy. The previous unification of England by the house of Wessex in the tenth century ensured that it fell rapidly to William, unlike the more lengthy processes by which the Iron Age and Romano-British kingdoms had fallen to Rome and the Anglo-Saxons respectively. The contrast with the Roman invasions of 55 and 54 BCE and, more conclusively, 43 CE is especially notable. When King Harold was defeated and killed at the battle of Hastings, England fell with him. William did not need to fight another battle. This was due in part to England's centralisation.

At the same time, the contingent nature of Continental links was strongly underlined by the other invasion of 1066, that by Harald Hardrada, king of Norway. Initially successful, this invasion was crushed at Stamford Bridge by the army under King Harold of England that was subsequently defeated at Hastings. The long-standing Viking political interest in England remained strong until the late eleventh century and in Scotland remained significant until the late thirteenth century.

William's seizure of the throne was followed by a social revolution, for the imposition of a new and foreign ruling order affected everybody. Peasants had to adapt to new landlords who spoke a different language and had onerous new demands. Not least in comparison with Cnut, the English were generally treated as a conquered people, and were turned into one remarkably fast. Though there was assimilation, not least through intermarriage, there was no lasting comparison with the Roman attempt to co-opt and Romanise local élites. Old institutions were used for the benefit of new rulers, with particular concepts of justice and government, and with novel problems, especially the defence of the duchy of Normandy from its neighbours, the king of France in particular. It is mistaken to see late Anglo-Saxon society and government as an unchanging world that was suddenly brutally disrupted by the Norman Conquest, but, nevertheless, there was a sweeping transformation.

The Conquest was not just a matter of political displacement. It also brought in a French-speaking élite as well as major changes in the organisation and content of English Christianity. New institutional developments in the Church were related to the imposition of a 'foreign' emphasis, although they also reflected the widespread movement for Church reform that characterised the late eleventh century.

English Exceptionalism?

Alongside aspects of continuity, the scale of devastation caused by the Conquest and the resistance to it, especially, but not only, the brutal 'Harrying of the North' in 1069–70, surpassed in its scale anything that had recently happened. This helped ensure that the conquest was a matter of force, violence, disruption and expropriation. It was only once Norman rule was established that the focus could shift to adaptability and continuity.

Alongside the political dimension, the essential characteristics of society were determined by environment, technological level and socio-cultural inheritance. These were not distinct to England but were shared, with some variations, with the Continent. This remained true of the Christian heritage, as well as of society as male-dominated, hierarchical, deferential and patriarchal. However, as such characteristics were not unique to Europe but, for example, loomed large in China, they cannot be used to define a distinctively European civilisation.

While stressing common features between Britain and the Continent, it is also pertinent to emphasise the regional, indeed local, dimension in both. For reasons and with results that sometimes last to the present, this point vitiates simple comparisons between England and the other parts of the British Isles, or between the latter and the Continent. There were different responses to the late Roman heritage, both within England/ Britain, and between there and the Continent. It is clear that sharing the same religion and inegalitarian social structure was compatible with marked social and cultural variations. So also for today: modern technology, capitalism and democracy still have very different consequences and resonances. Returning to medieval England, the localised nature of the agrarian economy was highly pronounced. Britain was divided into a large number of local economies, the interrelationships of which provided the dynamic of the national economy.

At the same time, environmental and ecological changes could be continent-wide or on a greater scale, as with the temperature cooling from the thirteenth century and the Black Death (plague) of 1346–53. There were also widespread technological changes, such as the spread of windmills, and the switch from oxen to faster and more adaptable horses for ploughing.

Arguments of English socio-economic exceptionalism come from this period, notably that society became distinctly and distinctively less stratified than those on the Continent, with a greater degree of freedom. Certainly, the broad lines of development were similar to those on the Continent. Population growth between *c.*900 and the early fourteenth century resulted, throughout Europe, in demand-led economic growth and the cultivation of new lands. Some were gained by drainage of marshland, most by clearing forests. This very process of expansion is still marked in the place names of Europe, including Britain, for it was in this period that most originated. The stress was on creation: Newcastle, Neuburg, Neuchâtel, Newport, Nieuport, etc., and the lasting names of resulting settlements. Trade grew, while road links were improved.

Economic development was expressed in an increased dependence on the market for food, as well as the partial replacement of wages in kind by wages in cash. In turn, the fourteenth century, like the seventeenth, saw a general recession, with population numbers declining (in the fourteenth century in particular due to the Black Death) and social discontent rising. The Peasants' Revolt of 1381 in England was paralleled on the Continent, while the heterodox Lollard movement in England had similarities to another heresy, that of the Hussites in Bohemia.

To be ahistorical, a Europe comprising regions each with an essentially similar heritage, which is the recent prospectus of some European enthusiasts concerned to lessen the grip of the nation state, can be discerned in the medieval period. At the same time, as England, let alone Britain, has never had a uniform economy, no more than France, Italy or other states have done, a stress on regional diversity, although valid, is not a complete answer to the question of national distinctiveness. Much of England certainly moved rapidly away from 'classical' feudalism, and towards a money economy. And yet, if throughout the British Isles society was becoming more complex, as the distribution of wealth broadened, and monetary transactions, the volume of the currency, trade, both domestic and foreign, specialisation in occupations, social mobility and literacy all increased, and industry spread into some rural areas, the same was also true of the Continent.

These very developments helped to foster links between Britain, more particularly England, and the Continent. Commercial relations grew and diversified, not least as a result of Italian and Hanseatic (North German) commercial activity. Economic links with France became more important after the Norman Conquest. Wool and cloth exports kept England's trade in balance, were vital to the government's finances, and helped to finance English participation in the Hundred Years War. The exports also ensured that England was concerned about the political situation in the Low Countries. Alongside common trends and links, however, there was a contrast between the spread of the money economy across at least much of England and the more traditional socio-economic practices over much of the Continent.

In religious and cultural terms, the Church ensured that there was an international European dimension to everything. At the battle of Hastings in 1066, William the Conqueror had a papal banner. From the time of the Second Crusade in the 1140s, there was also a prominent British, more particularly English, role in the Crusades. In that crusade, the English crusaders helped drive the Moors from Lisbon in 1147. As a part of Western Christendom, the English Church was legally subject to the Papacy, and was affected by ecclesiological changes such as the Investiture Contest and the Great Schism. Shifts in practice, such as the spread of new monastic orders, for example the Cistercians, and of the friars, affected Britain.

Moreover, British clerics followed careers in the Church outside Britain, Nicholas Breakspear becoming Pope Adrian IV (1154–9). A considerable number of Englishmen taught at the University of Paris, including Stephen Langton, who was made a Cardinal in 1206. King John refused to have Langton as Archbishop of Canterbury on the grounds that he had only dwelt among his enemies. This led, in 1208, to England being placed under an interdict by Innocent III: all church services were suspended. The following year, John was excommunicated, and, when he bought his peace with Innocent in 1213, he did so by making England a papal fief, although this was only temporary.

Proto-Nationalism?

John's dispute with the Papacy was only one of a number involving English monarchs. His father, Henry II, submitted to the Church in 1174 after the killing of Thomas Becket, Archbishop of Canterbury in 1170. This was a reflection of the damage to reputation the Church could inflict. These disputes broadened out into a general hostility to foreign ecclesiastical jurisdiction and to the movement of funds abroad. This process can be presented as proto-nationalism and as prefiguring modern tensions with Brussels, but it was far from unique to England. The rapid growth in papal pretensions from the late eleventh century, at a time when the papal curia (court), under a succession of lawyer popes, was becoming in effect the legal centre of Christendom and thus a prime source of papal authority and money, led to disputes throughout Western Christendom. These disputes helped in the formation of 'proto-national' churches and of a 'national' ecclesiastical consciousness, in which there was the idea and practice of hostility to 'foreign' clerics. Papal government also stimulated the development of indigenous government. The process of national ecclesiastical consciousness was furthered greatly during the Great Schism (1378–1417), because the universalism of papal government and Catholic identity was temporarily fractured.

Specific political issues had already led to tension. The hostility of successive Emperors to the pretensions and Italian interests of the Papacy affected the situation in Germany. Moreover, relations between England and the Papacy were complicated by the hostile English response to the papal position regarding England's conflicts with France and Scotland.

There was a clear tension over loyalty within the Church in England, one that focused in particular on papal taxation and patronage. For example, in 1231, there was a widespread movement against alien absentees, especially Italians, who had been presented by the Pope to English benefices (Church positions). The use of the term 'alien' reflected a sense of foreignness. Papal appointments to these benefices were often simply an award of an income to a foreign cleric.

Such opposition was part of a more widespread antagonism throughout society to strangers, to everyone who was not known. This ensured that 'foreigners' included 'internal' outsiders, people from other settlements or regions. Thus, as today, nationalism could overlap with regionalism and localism. As a particularly acute form of antagonism, anti-Semitism flourished on the Continent from the time of the First Crusade in the 1090s and in England from the early twelfth century. It reflected a hostility to aliens that was a readily apparent feature of medieval society. Under Edward I, the Jews were expelled from England in 1290, a measure that theoretically remained in force until 1655.

In England, there was also to be hostility to Italians, Flemings, French, Welsh, Irish and Scots. Possibly the hostility to foreigners is a matter of a more defined consciousness arising from the state development of Western Europe. Much, however, may be due to an increase in evidence of hostility, to the greater concern of government with civil violence and the swelling volume of records of crime and litigation, and to the growing awareness of wealth, stemming in part from a rise in international trade.

Again prefiguring the situation today, with some rejectionist critics of the European Union seeing themselves as committed Europeans, there was loyalty to medieval Christendom but not always to its practices. The contradictory relations that this situation could lead to were demonstrated by Robert Grosseteste, Bishop of Lincoln from 1235 to 1253, apparently a bitter opponent of granting benefices to foreign clerics who Innocent IV allegedly dreamed had given him an incurable wound. Grosseteste therefore can be presented in 'nationalist' terms, but, looked at closely, he becomes more complex, in a pattern that may be highlighted when later historians come to look at the present day. Grosseteste was opposed not to the appointment of foreigners per se to English benefices but, rather, to that of unworthy clerics. Furthermore, he praised the university course at Paris, was the first rector of the Franciscans, an international order, at Oxford, and sought Innocent's support in his own dispute with the chapter at Lincoln.

Britain was very much part of Europe culturally, and unsurprisingly so, as the principal sources of patronage were all international: the monarchy, the Church and the greater nobility. Architects and musicians worked in cosmopolitan settings and styles. For example, England's very distinctive Decorated style of architecture of *c*.1270–1350 was an adaptation of the French Gothic. The key building in England was Henry III's rebuilt Westminster Abbey, which was heavily indebted stylistically to two French exemplars: Rheims Cathedral and the Sainte-Chapelle in Paris. The shift in style in England, especially in the design of window tracery, was a response to the novelty of Westminster. The University of Paris very much influenced those of Cambridge and Oxford.

It is possible to sketch out an element of divergence, focusing, in particular, on the development of vernacular (English or Scots as opposed to French or Latin) literature. This led to major works such as, in England, the anonymous *Sir Gawain and the Green Knight*, Geoffrey Chaucer's *Canterbury Tales* (*c*.1387), William Langland's *Piers Plowman* (1362–92) and Thomas Malory's *Le Morte d'Arthur* (1469), as well as ballads, carols and mystery plays. Nevertheless, most literature continued to be written in Latin. Rather than thinking of the languages in terms of rivalry, although that element could exist, it is better to consider them as having particular functions. The vernacular could be important as an expression of national consciousness, but the relationship between language and nationalism was complex. Indeed, the vernacular could serve for the transmission of cosmopolitan ideas and an international consciousness, as well as for criticism of both.

Moreover, it is far from clear that specific medieval artistic styles had either any political reverberations or any relationship with proto-nationalism. The Perpendicular, a native architectural style of the fourteenth and fifteenth centuries, was recognisably different from such Continental forms as the French Flamboyant Gothic and the Portuguese Manueline style, but, at the same time, it was part of a common trend in which the Gothic went out in a blaze of glory, and therefore can be better seen as a school rather than a distinctive movement. The Perpendicular, like the style of English music developed by composers such as William Cornish, John Dunstable and Walter Frye, attracted Continental interest and was influential abroad. Furthermore, Chaucer was influenced by Continental works, such as Boccaccio's *Decameron*.

Thus, the British Isles in the later medieval period were still very much part of an international cultural world. The relationship, nevertheless, was different in type from that of the Norman and Angevin period when Continental, especially French, influences had been dominant. If, by the fifteenth century, there was any doubt of the vitality of English culture, it was as part of, and not in opposition to, a wider Western European cultural world.

The law was one sphere of obvious contrast. In England, it developed, especially from the twelfth century, into a system of common law that was distinctive in both the content of the law and the way in which it was administered. The legal system reflected the particular imprint of interested monarchs, especially Henry II and Edward I, and the nature of what was, by contemporary Western European standards, a sophisticated administrative system that owed much to the strength of Norman and Angevin monarchical power. English common law had links with what was going on abroad, but was also a distinctive unity, and that at a time when Roman law was coming back into fashion on the Continent.

English common law was especially committed to the protection of rights and liberties, and encouraged a respect for the autonomy of individual thought and action. In combination with the early emergence of an institutional monarchy, this was particularly responsible for the character and continuity of English political society. As a result, the spread within the EU of the authority of European courts and legal concepts is significant.

The Legacies of War

The crucial political legacy of Norman England (1066–1154) was of war stemming from continuous confrontation with a neighbouring state. After 1066, England was part of a polity that spanned the Channel, one that found itself obliged to ward off the ambitions of other expanding territories, most significantly the kingdom of France. The continuous military effort that this entailed was to be a central theme, instrumental both in the development of government and in the domestic political history of the period, just as conflict played a comparable role elsewhere in Europe. Although the Anglo-Norman realms were, both in origin and in development, less a single state than a fortuitous conglomeration that had little in common in administrative or legal terms, they were given common political direction by the interests of their ruler.

This continued throughout the Middle Ages, as the Anglo-Norman inheritance was expanded with new dynasties and acquisitions. The Anglo-Norman 'empire' fell to bits in the civil war of Stephen's reign, and the Angevin 'empire', of which England formed a part after 1154, was a new and different creation. There was a degree of assimilation between England and Normandy in the days of Norman rule, but none under the Angevins. Each constituent unit of the Angevins' dominions was ruled according to its own local laws and customs.

Five kings—William I, Henry I, Henry II, Richard I and Henry V—died in France where they were struggling to protect or strengthen their position. So also with heirs, such as Henry the Young King, the eldest surviving son of Henry II. Normandy and Anjou were both lost to France in 1203–4, which loosened the link between England and the French world. Aquitaine, which was left, was happy to retain the English link because it was a means of keeping rule from Paris at bay. When Philip

Augustus of France conquered Normandy, he told the Anglo-Norman nobility there that they would have to choose: if they stayed loyal to John, then they would forfeit their lands south of the Channel. John responded with a like ultimatum. Although a few highly cosmopolitan families, such as the de Valences, were present in the later thirteenth century, they were the exceptions that proved the rule. It is difficult to speak of a cross-Channel aristocracy after the 1220s.

French military intervention in England after 1215 was a logical consequence of the post-Conquest cross-Channel nature of the English monarchy. Whereas previous invasions of England had been motivated by a desire for wealth and land, it was now plausible to attack England, or to support its rivals within the British Isles, in order to undermine the policy of England's monarchs, specifically their defence of their Continental interests.

The invasion was defeated in 1217, but, as a cross-current, under Henry III (r. 1216–72), there was a hostility to foreigners in the shape of the king's foreign favourites. From 1258, hostility to aliens played a crucial role in the attempt to limit royal authority. Political society was becoming increasingly anglicised even though the monarchy continued with its bolder, broader ambitions. This was very much seen in the ambitions of Edward III (r. 1327–77) and Henry V (r. 1413–22) in the Hundred Years War in France (1337–1453).

At the same time, as with other interventions, this conflict indicated the extent to which England was part of Europe in the form of having allies as well as commitments. The successes of the kings of England owed much to the existence of French allies, and the Hundred Years War was in part an international dimension of a series of French civil wars. There was also a pattern of interaction with international relations in the Low Countries, Germany and Iberia. The implications for England were many. Henry V wished to absorb the leadership of

Christendom in so far as it was held by the French. This played a role in the anxiety of Parliament about keeping the two crowns separate and not becoming a satellite of France.

Yet, just over three decades after Henry's death from dysentery in 1422, France was lost as a result of repeated military failure. Calais was held until 1558, the claim to the French throne was only abandoned in 1802, and the Channel Islands are still held, but the Norman duchy, the Angevin empire and Lancastrian France had all gone.

A sense of national consciousness was not dependent on this failure. Indeed, the involvement in France had arguably forwarded, rather than delayed, the development of a 'national' state, encouraging xenophobia, royal war propaganda, military service, national taxation and the related expansion of the role of Parliament. As on other occasions, war had helped create a sense of 'us' and 'them', a sense that was important to identity. A pre-Reformation, 'national' Church had also crystallised in the context of papal claims and of royal and other resistance to them. At the same time, the vitality of late-medieval English Catholicism had very much to do with its being part of an international Church.

Political events, notably in the shape of the unpredictabilities of warfare, were important. Overlapping jurisdictions, a cross-border aristocracy, and England's place within the Plantagenet amalgamation of distinctive territories had all inhibited the political consequences of a national consciousness. Thus, the total defeat of the attempt on the French throne was of great consequence.

The more insular, even at times and in some aspects isolationist, character of both England and the policies of its monarchs after 1453 and, even more, 1558 was to be one of the keys to its subsequent domestic and international development. By then, England lacked any tradition on which a standing army or a permanent system of taxation could be built. Royal demands for help in war, and the often clear-cut opposition to them, had both been accommodated in a limited monarchy, with Parliament serving as a national political focus. In its early stages, although crucially it was the representative assembly of the entire kingdom and not of a part of it, Parliament was no different, to any great extent, from its Continental counterparts. However, the frequent need to raise taxation to pay for warfare led to Parliament becoming more powerful.

Furthermore, in later-medieval England, there was an emphasis on constitutional and political contrast with France. It was argued, in a language that was to be long-standing, that there was a distinction between the free and prosperous English, who supported the Crown because it gave good government, and the abject French, who were compelled into political obedience. Thus, Sir John Fortescue, in the 1470s, in his *Governance of England: otherwise called The Difference between an Absolute and a Limited Monarchy*, 'singled out the quality of collegiality of crown and subjects as the essence of the English political system, something that distinguished it from France'. The former he described as a *dominium politicum et regale*, the latter as *dominium regale*. Whereas in England government required the co-operation of a free political society, in France there were no effective institutional checks, such as parliamentary assent to legislation and taxation.

National consciousness can face the same fate as the 'bourgeoisie': forever rising in the assessment of historians. In practice, there were still powerful international and cosmopolitan forces and tendencies in the fifteenth century. Yet, the loss of the French empire of the kings of England helped make England different from the Continental dynasties, notably the Habsburgs, the Valois, the Aragonese and the Vasa, that sought to create far-flung territorial empires in Western Europe. Moreover, the death of the Hungarian king Louis II, when his army was totally destroyed at the battle of Mohács (1526) by the invading Ottoman (Turkish) army of Süleyman the Magnificent, also took the Habsburgs into Eastern Europe. During the Italian Wars that began in 1494, the Valois sought to establish themselves in Italy as well, albeit unsuccessfully so.

The Late-Medieval State and Nation

At the same time, alongside such dynastic imperialism, there was a tendency to seek to consolidate authority in what was subsequently termed the new monarchies, a group that included England, Scotland and France. Frontiers became more defined and border zones were diminished. State bureaucracies tended to become more assertive. More generally, alongside comparisons between Britain and Western Europe, it is pertinent to note the contrasts. These emphasise the degree to which the Continent was not a unity that could be readily compared with Britain or England.

Across Europe, proximity to centres of power, such as London, the Île de France and the Scottish Central Lowlands, brought a greater awareness of the political reality of England, France and Scotland than life in many regions that were far from economically and politically marginal. However, at the same time, Border ballads, such as 'Johnnie Armstrong', suggest that the consciousness of Scottish identity could be very high in the Borders. Indeed, the later Middle Ages witnessed an expansion of the area of governmental effectiveness, and a strengthening of the idea of national patriotism. This was part of the process that England (and Scotland) shared with the Continent, but also differentiated it from elsewhere.

Other differences were readily apparent. In England, the Norman and Angevin kings were representatives of a type of monarchy in which the king was, first and foremost, 'lord', and then administrator of a mass of wealth and power, rather than, like the Capetian kings of France, deriving his power from atavistic roots in tribe and nation, which laid an emphasis on the holiness of the king's person. The failure by the Norman and Angevin kings to create a permanent, stable, trans-Channel polity interacted with the development of national consciousness in England.

Crucially, a sense of political community, headed by the king, but to which he could be held accountable, lay behind the political and constitutional developments of the thirteenth century: Magna Carta and its reissues, the powerful baronial movement towards the close of Henry III's reign, and the criticism of Edward I in the 1290s, criticism focused in Parliament. Politically, England was no longer simply part of a trans-Channel dynastic amalgam. A sense of political community was institutionalised in Parliament, which, unlike the royal court, did not represent the full extent of the monarch's possessions and connections. It was in Parliament that hostility to 'alien' influences, whether political, ecclesiastical or commercial, was voiced most clearly. There was no doubt that it was possible to distinguish aliens from the English, and also that, in Parliament, institutional means existed to give voice and effect to their views and to do so on behalf of a nation.

A growth of national consciousness and a sharpening of perceptions were not, however, dependent on the development of the authority of the unitary state. Thus, the stronger consciousness of Germanness and German nationhood evolved in a very different political context from that of England. It has been argued that nationalism was a concept developed in the French Revolutionary–Napoleonic period and thereafter, and that the sense of collective identity which existed within the earlier framework of the monarchical state took a different form from that to be found in the nineteenth-century nation state.

However, rather than marrying nationalism to modernity, nationalism can also be seen earlier in terms of communities. In medieval England, nationality was defined not so much by biological characteristics as by law, custom, dress, personal habits and similar characteristics that people of different ethnic backgrounds could share. Such a definition of nationhood is one that can be employed in the later Middle Ages to distinguish nations and, in parts of Europe, nation states.[1]

More generally, a 'zero sum' model, in which a national consciousness could be developed and sustained only at the expense of other competing consciousnesses, local, regional and international—a form of 'loyalty oath' approach to the past—is inappropriate, a point that remains relevant. In practice, there was a diversity of consciousness, identity and allegiance. A language of national identity and interest, nation being understood primarily as the subjects of a particular kingdom (rather than of an individual king who might be the ruler of several), was an aspect of relations at such a level of political, economic and ecclesiastical activity. However, in general, in England activity at the national level did not clash with other aspects of political consciousness. There were obvious areas of contention, not least over the international dimensions of ecclesiastical activity, and the policies and regional strength of leading magnates. Yet, England was scarcely unique in this.

At the same time, precisely because it was relatively compact, and certainly so compared to France, Spain and the Germanic lands, it was easier to focus on national rather than regional identity and for both government and politics to operate as national forces and in accordance with national trends. The problems that were posed when trying to take this forward on a wider scale are instructive. Thus, in Wales, English rulers encountered rebellions, most seriously that of Owen Glendower in the 1400s. Resistance in Ireland restricted English control to a portion of the island. In Scotland, there was complete failure despite repeated efforts from the 1290s to the mid-fourteenth century. These contrasts were not solely a matter of contingent political and military events nor, indeed, inevitable in the maw of geopolitics. Instead, there was a degree to which developing concepts, whether or not called nationalist or proto-nationalist, could have a significant political impact. This was also very much to be the case in the sixteenth and seventeenth centuries.

Again, the situation today offers parallels, although the context of modern discussion of European identities and links is one in which other international models and pressures also play a role. In the medieval period, there was no equivalent to the United States, while China, although the most powerful state in the world, did not press on the British economy.

2

FROM THE REFORMATION TO THE
GLORIOUS REVOLUTION, 1533–1688

The defiance of Continental authority and power rings clearly from the sixteenth and seventeenth centuries. This period was, and is, noted for a series of actions that were each, in a way, acts of defiance towards such powers, notably that of the Papacy and of the crowns of France and Spain. Key episodes include the English and Scottish Reformations; the defeat of the Spanish Armada in 1588; and the 'Glorious Revolution' of 1688–9. The last saw the rejection, with James II (r. 1685–8), James VII of Scotland, of Popery and the alleged principles of Continental absolutism.

The Reformation definitely played a key role in the assertion of a national consciousness—separately so for England and Scotland. England acquired, in the Church of England, a distinctive ecclesiastical path and a distinctive church; an institution with a branch in every parish teaching loyalty to the English state. The pretensions and powers of the Westminster Parliament were enhanced as a result of the Reformation and, thereafter, maintained. Subsequently, England took parliamentary government further forward, episodically in the 1640s and 1650s and, in combination with the monarch, after 1688.

Separately and later, England became a trans-oceanic commercial and colonial power and developed a permanent professional royal navy, supported by a whole department of state. In contrast, after the loss of the French territories, which had a last aftershock in 1558 with the fall of Calais to French assault, England was insular, as far as the Continent was concerned, to a degree that had not been true for centuries. Her rulers were less important in Western European diplomacy than had been the case from the Norman Conquest. More significantly, despite the gain of Dunkirk, Gibraltar and Minorca, the first only temporarily, the concern with Continental possessions and pretensions proved of scant consequence between the accession of Elizabeth I in 1558 and that of the Hanoverian dynasty in 1714. Moreover, the territorial interests of the Hanoverians in modern Germany were seen as foreign by much of the political nation.

Religion and Politics

And yet, the rulers and political élite of England were bound closely to Continental affairs, in some respects more so than in the late fifteenth century. The Reformation ensured both an independent English Church and also new religious links with Protestant Northern Europe. It was impossible, theologically and politically, to be 'Catholic without the Pope', and the inconsistencies in Henry VIII's position were laid bare by his difficulties in fixing the present, let alone the future under his children, three of whom succeeded him.

Furthermore, English foreign policy now acquired a religious dimension. From the 1550s, as it became apparent that the Catholic Church and its allies were striking back, so a sense of community of interests with Protestants abroad developed rapidly.

The 1560s saw the outbreak of confessional violence in France and then the Low Countries, and English troops intervened from the 1560s and 1580s respectively.

As a result of Lollardy, a heterodox movement in the late fourteenth and early fifteenth centuries, translation of the Bible into English had been associated with heresy, and in the sixteenth century the language was still considered too 'rude' and 'barbarous' for the sacred text. In contrast, as a consequence of the Reformation, English was to become the language of God's word in Britain. This was an important new dynamic in the relationships between England, on the one hand, and Scotland and Wales, on the other, although William Morgan's translation of the entire Bible into Welsh was published in 1588. This might appear a linguistic counterforce to the Protestant national theme but, instead, reflects the pluralistic nature of nationhood at this time.

The Reformation had many cross-currents in its influence. One important link with the Continent resulted from the immigration of Protestant refugees from elsewhere in Europe. Located mostly in southern towns, such as London, Norwich and Canterbury, most continued to look to the Continent and provided an important means for the transmission of new developments. The arrival of these refugees, and their presence in distinct communities, were the cause of a measure of popular xenophobia and, separately, official concern. In the 1630s, William Laud, Archbishop of Canterbury, sought, unsuccessfully, to force children born to immigrant parents in England to join the Church of England, although he was successful in the case of grandchildren. Nevertheless, the persistence of Huguenot (French Protestant) communities was in some respects misleading, for many immigrants appear to have married English spouses, most of their offspring were absorbed into English society in the second generation, and only a small minority attended Huguenot services for several generations.

This remained the case after another large-scale Huguenot immigration that was launched in 1685 by Louis XIV's unilateral revocation of Protestant rights in France, a measure that was followed with close attention in Britain. The 1708 Foreign Protestant Naturalisation Act permitted naturalisation of any foreign Protestant who swore the Oath of Allegiance and took the Anglican sacrament. Repealed in 1711, this was replaced by an Act that naturalised all British citizens born abroad, a measure that was to be important to the nature of the empire. There was scant equivalent to the later, long-term establishment of large and distinct Muslim communities.

After Elizabeth's accession to the throne of England in 1558, some Catholics, mostly from higher social groups, left for the Continent, while others sent their children there to be educated. Moreover, the imposition of the Elizabethan Acts of Supremacy and Uniformity in Ireland led the 'Old English' settlers to ally with the native Irish in defence of Catholicism. The English and Irish Catholic diasporas were a source and means for plans for the reconversion of England, and such plans came to play a role in the rivalry between Elizabethan England and Philip II's Spain.

Religion played a key part. The strategic problems confronting Elizabeth's ministers, especially the French in Scotland at the outset of her reign, and later the Spaniards in Ireland, ensured in England a new focus on a united British Isles. Indeed, the 'British Question' was in large part one of Anglo-Continental relations, even more notably so after the Reformation. The acceptance of the Reformation by Scotland and Wales was crucial to their integration into a British consciousness and policy.

Ireland, however, rejected the Reformation, and was far more unstable than either Scotland or Wales in the sixteenth and seventeenth centuries. Indeed, the different religion and, to a considerable extent, language of the Irish played a major role in the depersonalising of them in the minds of the English and Scots.

The refusal of most of the Irish to accept the Reformation was key to the politics of the period and also central to the divergence of Ireland from the general model of British development.

The struggles of the late sixteenth century encouraged, in both England and Scotland, the conflation of a sense of national independence with both anti-Catholicism and hostility to the major Continental Catholic powers. As with other episodes in which national consciousness and a rhetoric of national interest were advanced, these actually served a partisan purpose, for national consciousness was defined against domestic, as much as foreign, opponents, and this gave that consciousness a particular political force and urgency. Thus, in England, as in Scotland, Catholics could be presented as supporters of hostile foreign powers, while these same powers appeared more threatening precisely because of their apparent (as well as real) support within Britain; and uncertainty over the royal succession made the combination even more threatening.

The result of the Reformation was therefore division and civil strife, a political world of conspiracy, the search for assistance from foreign co-religionists, and regional, social and factional differences exacerbated by confessional antagonism. Religion proved a spur for the development of resistance theories and practices, and it was a political world in which everything was seen to be at stake because of the prospect of state-directed religious change.

Religious and political fears and concerns fused in opposition to Spain. War with Spain from 1585 to 1604, which followed two decades of deteriorating relations, fostered national consciousness. Popular allegiance to Protestantism grew, and new national days of celebration recalling England's recent Protestant history became popular. Church bells were rung every 17 November to mark Elizabeth's accession. Her accession anniversary achieved totemic status. In 1682, the Council of Six planned a rising against Charles II that would coincide with the anniversary celebrations, and in London it was hoped that this would provide popular support for the rising.

Gunpowder Plot bonfires were to take place after 1605 to commemorate the thwarting of a Catholic conspiracy to destroy king and Parliament. English national culture was both becoming and being formed as a Protestant culture, and this long resonated as history and identity were joined. It is indicative of the change in national culture that in 2017 the BBC broadcast *Gunpowder*, a mini-series that provided a highly misleading account of the context and events of the period, one that was overly sympathetic to the conspirators.

The first of the Stuart rulers of England, James I (r. 1603–25), James VI of Scotland (r. 1567–1625), was a peacemaker who defused many of the tensions of Elizabeth's last years. In domestic terms, his was also the most peaceful reign since that of Edward III (r. 1327–77). This period of peace was followed by unsuccessful wars with Spain (1624–30) and France (1627–9), which greatly damaged the prestige of Charles I (r. 1625–49) and led to domestic political difficulties. At the same time, the contrast between the situation in the early 1630s and that during and after similar episodes of failure in the late-medieval period was evidence of the development of the political community, certainly in England, away from a near-automatic response of confrontation and the threat of violence.

Nevertheless, the extent to which Britain was still seen as a part of Europe, was affected by developments on the Continent and was seen in that light by contemporaries, was to be demonstrated abundantly during the reigns of James I and Charles I. James was criticised for allegedly pro-Spanish policies, and pressure to intervene on behalf of co-religionists in the Thirty Years War (1618–48) played a role in the wars with Spain and France, and also in the participation of many individuals in the struggle on the

Continent. The press owed much of its inception to reporting on the struggle.[1] The popular rejoicings that followed the failure of the proposed Spanish marriage for the future Charles I, in 1623, indicated the interrelationships of religion, domestic politics and international relations. The 1624 Parliament provided the basis for war with Spain, helping to channel popular and political enthusiasm for the conflict to effect. Two years later, Sir Dudley Digges told the Commons of 'a potent league made by the Popish parties against the Protestants'. About one-sixth of the army of Gustavus Adolphus of Sweden that fought in Germany in 1630–2 were Scots. Gustavus, whose activities were followed with great attention in Britain, was regarded as the Protestant champion, a role neither James nor Charles sought to fill, although James's eldest son, Prince Henry, and his son-in-law Frederick, Elector Palatine, did.

The major Scottish participation in the Thirty Years War helps to explain why Scotland contributed the most successful military element in the political crisis that began in 1638 and provided an important force in the subsequent civil war in England, certainly the key element until the laborious process of replacing the earlier parliamentary forces with a trained New Model Army had been completed. It was the ability of the Scots to defeat Charles I in the Bishops' Wars (1639–40) that led to the unravelling of his personal rule in England.

The Scots, like the English Parliamentarians who opposed Charles, were in large part acting against what they saw as crypto-Catholicism at home and its alignment with Catholicism abroad. For many, maybe most, British Protestants, there was no doubt that there was a mid-seventeenth-century crisis, a crisis whose cause, course and consequences were primarily religious, and one in which Britain was ultimately involved.

The struggle on the Continent, however, also left British politicians free to pursue their own conflicts with little foreign intervention. When one power was dominant in Northern Europe, it was able to intervene in English domestic affairs or British geopolitics, as France had done during the minority of Henry III and during the Wars of the Roses, and was to do again during the reign of Charles II in part due to the king's inconsistent policies, notably towards France and the United Provinces (Netherlands). In contrast, when there was no such hegemony, it was possible to push through domestic changes with a minimum of outside intervention. This was the experience of the Henrician and Edwardian Reformations, and was again that of the 1640s and 1650s.

All too often, the mutual rivalries of the Continental powers could not be relied upon. This was true for much of the 1530s, and crucially during the period of acute French weakness from 1559 until 1594 as the result of civil wars known as the French Wars of Religion, a period of Spanish strength and threat to both England and France. This situation was to recur and be readily apparent with France under the Revolutionaries and Napoleon, and with Germany in the early twentieth century.

The relationship was a complex one during the seventeenth century. Far from there being any English sense that Continental quarrels permitted independent solutions to England's problems, important aspects of political culture and national feeling derived from attitudes and acts of defiance by an embattled people. Indeed, at the one level, the civil wars in the British Isles were part of the European Wars of Religion. At the same time, Britain certainly benefited in the 1630s from peace and neutrality at a time when most of Europe was involved in the trauma of the Thirty Years War.

Exceptionalism and Similarities

At this point, it is clearly possible to point to differences between Britain and the Continent. These included the distinctive nature of the Church of England, the size and importance of London, the role of the common law, the small size of the army, and the consequences of being an island state. The common law tradition was significant for legal, intellectual and political divergence between England and the Roman law that was prevalent on the Continent. The jury system ensured popular participation in justice. London promoted the interaction of bourgeois and aristocratic thinking and values and the influence of commercial considerations upon national policy. Such diverse developments as England's commercial expansion and financial development, the flowering of drama in the Elizabethan and Jacobean period, and the defeat of the Crown in the Civil War cannot be understood without reference to London's central role in the political, economic and cultural life of the country.

Yet, alongside contrasts, it is also possible to stress parallels and similarities. Britain was a 'multiple' kingdom, like many Continental states, notably Spain, an inegalitarian society in which inherited control of property was crucial to political, social and economic authority and power, and a dynastic monarchy. She was far from unique in founding colonies abroad. The pull across the Atlantic and to the Indian Ocean that characterised England in the Elizabethan and Stuart period was, if anything, even more developed in Iberia (Portugal and Spain) and the Dutch Republic, as well as being seen in France. These pulls were not apparent in Scotland.

From a comparative perspective, it is pertinent to stress the unpredictable nature of political developments and the role of chance—for Continental states as well as Britain. For example, one of the most notable features of Elizabeth's reign was her longevity. Ruler for 44 years, she was the longest-reigning monarch since Edward III. This provided an opportunity for the consolidation of the Elizabethan Church settlement, the development of a measure of political stability, and the establishment of a generally acceptable Protestant succession. Elizabeth was the longest-living English monarch hitherto; she was not to be surpassed until George III (r. 1760–1820). Had she lived only as long as her mother or her half-brother, Edward VI, Elizabeth would never have become queen. If she had emulated her half-sister, Mary I, or her father, Henry VIII, she would have died before Mary, Queen of Scots. The comparative perspective in this respect offers a ready contrast with France, where a series of short reigns was linked to the assassinations of Henry III in 1589 and Henry IV in 1610. Other key examples of chance included the death of James I's oldest son, Prince Henry, and the fact that Charles II had no legitimate sons, and that the Catholic James II, a monarch without skill, therefore came to the throne in 1685. The absence of direct heirs of Mary II and of Anne was also important.

There were significant similarities between British and Continental society. Whatever the constitutional system and the determination and good fortune of individual rulers, it was the major landholders who dominated politics and government, especially the crucial role of the localities. This basic continuity was as fundamental to the history of the period as the discontinuities represented by religious change and political events. The crucial political relationships, in Britain and on the Continent, were those of central government and the nobility. The latter owned and controlled most of the land and were the local notables, enjoying social prestige and effective governmental control of the localities.

Central government meant in practice, whether in England or France, the monarch and a very small group of advisors and officials. The notion that they were capable of creating the basis of a modern state is misleading. There were not the mechanisms to intervene effectively and consistently in the localities, nor the information necessary for effective planning. Without reliable or

often any information concerning population, revenues, economic activity or landownership, and lacking land surveys and
reliable and detailed maps, governments operated in what was, by
modern standards, an information void. This situation did not
really change until the nineteenth century. In Britain, this century was marked by institutions and practices, notably the establishment and sustaining of the Ordnance Survey and the intro-
duction of the decennial census, that rested on a high degree of
public acceptance of governmental power.

Lacking the reach of modern governments, those of the early
modern period relied on other bodies and individuals to fulfil
many functions that are now discharged by central government,
and these bodies and individuals reflected the interests, ideology
and personnel of the social élite. Whatever the rhetoric and constitutional nature of authority, the reality of power was decen-
tralised and symbiotic, and therefore consensual in so far as relations between Crown and élite were concerned.

The nature of the consensus, however, varied, chronologically,
geographically and socially. It could be particularly difficult to
create and sustain a consensus in frontier regions or in subordinate parts of multiple kingdoms, for example Ireland. This was
especially the case if major changes were introduced, most obviously with the Reformation. Thus, the Dutch Revolt against the
rule of Philip II of Spain can be compared with the Nine Years
War in Ireland in 1594–1603. Both crises began with disputes
over established liberties and were greatly exacerbated by religious differences and foreign intervention.

Both in Britain and the Continent, monarchs were not primarily administrative modernisers. Instead, as with their medieval predecessors, there was a more variegated situation. Respect
for, and co-operation with, the views, interests and ethos of
established élites could be matched by breakdowns in co-operation, which were frequently accompanied by initiatives to expand

royal policy. These became more common as a result of the Reformation Crisis. The new experience of widespread religious differences exacerbated anxieties and disputes within countries and, on the part of the state, accentuated the desire for governmental control.

In Britain, as on the Continent, social welfare and organised mass health care and education, in so far as they existed, were largely the responsibility of ecclesiastical institutions, lay bodies with religious connections, or other local lay bodies. The regulation of urban commerce and manufacturing was largely left to town governments. The 'farming out' (subcontracting, 'outsourcing' or privatising) of a wide range of activities that would later be seen as natural activities of government, such as the raising of taxes and troops, was a characteristic practice. The administration of the localities, and notably of law and order there, was commonly left to the local notables, whatever the formal mechanisms and institutions of their authority. The reality, in Britain and on the Continent, was self-government of the localities by their notables and, at the national level, a political system that was largely run by the propertied.

The key to stable government was to ensure that the local notables governed in accordance with the wishes of the centre, but this was largely achieved by giving them the instructions that they sought. For the notables, it was essential both that they received such instructions and that they received a fair share of governmental patronage. This system worked, and its cohesion, if not always harmony, was maintained not so much by formal bureaucratic mechanisms, as by the patronage and clientage networks that linked local notables to those wielding national influence and enjoying access to the monarch. In England, the gentry, as justices of the peace, were the crucial figures, and the practice of government was closely linked to an effective politics, not least because gentry MPs dominated the House of Commons.

Moreover, compared to the Continent, the gentry were not greatly under the control of the nobility.

Aside from the functional similarity between Britain and the Continent, there was an ideological counterpart in the form of a shared belief in the rule of law and in governments being subject to it. The constitutional mechanisms by which this operated varied. Nevertheless, there was a common opposition to despotism, which was generally conceptualised as unchristian and as the policy of Oriental or Classical tyrants, such as the Ottoman sultans or the Roman emperor Nero. In this, as in other respects, there were many similarities in the political languages employed in both Britain and the Continent.

There was also a common economic trajectory. Both Britain and the Continent were affected by sixteenth-century growth and by seventeenth-century problems, whether demographic stagnation, deflation or an end to growth. Though the weight placed upon individual explanatory factors, such as sunspots and a 'Little Ice Age' in the seventeenth century, or changes in the supply of bullion from Spanish South America, has varied, they all share the common characteristic of European-wide, indeed global, applicability. Britain was closely linked to the European international economy. English cloth exports accounted for about 30 per cent of the value of Antwerp's trade in its heyday, and jobs and customs revenues greatly depended on this trade. Transoceanic exploration brought new trades—with North America, the West Indies, West Africa and India. Nevertheless, the most important growth in English exports in the seventeenth century was first to Spain and later to Portugal and Italy.

Any stress on cultural links between Britain and the Continent may appear more surprising, given the role of religious division, but, again, there were common features, such as stylistic tendencies and modes of patronage. The Classics were a common inheritance for the European élite, and British patrons avidly purchased Continental works and supported foreign artists. Charles I was very impressed, on his visit to Spain in 1623 in pursuit of his plan for a marriage with the daughter of Philip IV, by the image of monarchy portrayed in the works of Rubens, Titian and Velázquez, and commissioned and purchased accordingly. Charles's cultural vision was very much in line with that of royal patrons of the arts on the Continent, such as Philip IV and Louis XIII.

More generally, intellectual links with Italy were sustained. However, in the crucial world of print, relations with the United Provinces (Dutch Republic), with its active and relatively free publishing industry, were of greater importance. This provided an instance of the interplay of similarities and differences. The similarity between England and the United Provinces was, at one level, most clearly between London and Amsterdam. At another level, and looking towards the early eighteenth century, England, like the United Provinces and Hamburg, was to have a relatively free press, but this was not the case elsewhere on the Continent.

It is frequently claimed that a common cultural pattern can be detected from the late sixteenth century in both Protestant and Catholic Europe in the shape of an assault on popular culture from the new moral didacticism of Protestant and post-Tridentine Catholic ecclesiastical and secular authorities. New intellectual and artistic fashions and codes of behaviour are held to have corroded the loyalty of the upper and middling orders to traditional beliefs and pastimes, marginalising a formerly common culture and pushing it down the social scale. Thus, once attention moves away from discourses of hostility, it is possible to focus on common characteristics.

A stress on common characteristics at this point invites the questions of whether England nevertheless did follow a different trajectory from the Continental states and, if so, whether it did this as a consequence of distinctive characteristics or thanks to chance factors. The medieval inheritance for England was that of a relatively compact territory and an effective monarchy, as well as a common legal code, and a common political assembly at Westminster. Compactness and strength: the two in combination can be used to explain a degree of national consciousness that contrasted with a stronger regionalism on the Continent. This contrast has been associated with the development of a national Parliament, in contrast to the regional estates of, most obviously, France, a state, like Spain, that was far larger than England or Scotland.

The argument requires some qualification. At the British level, there was no compactness to match that of England. Wales was not incorporated into Parliament, the shrieval system and the English legal system until the very one-sided Acts of Union of 1536–43. Norse law was not abolished in Orkney and Shetland until 1611. The accession of James VI of Scotland to the English throne in 1603 led to no Act of Union. Thus, most observations made about English distinctiveness are not pertinent at the British scale. Indeed, much of the political history of 1637–1707 can be regarded as an attempt to work out a political solution to this diversity. Failure in Scotland forced Charles I to turn to the Westminster Parliament in 1640 in order to obtain financial support.

This episode drew on an important strand of English history. The development of Parliament during the reigns of Edward I (1272–1307) and Edward III (1327–77) owed much to the conflicts of the period: England's international situation was directly affecting her domestic politics. War could not pay for itself, and the king could only be independent of Parliament if war was avoided. The use of parliamentary pressure to influence the composition and objectives of government was an inevitable consequence. Parliament could also serve as a means for eliciting support and obtaining funds for royal policies, but the resulting development of corporate identity and continuity also affected the freedom of political manoeuvre that monarchs enjoyed.

The English and Scottish monarchies had not gained wealth as a result of the explosion of European trans-oceanic activity at the close of the fifteenth and beginning of the sixteenth centuries. English expeditions failed to discover a North-West or a North-East passage to Asia and also missed out on the compensation of American bullion. English commercial penetration of the Indian Ocean only began after the Portuguese were well established there. Thus, resources remained a serious problem for the Crown, although it was scarcely unique in this among European states. Indeed, much of the administrative and political history of the period is a question of different strategies of indebtedness, their causes and consequences.

Yet, as so often, it is necessary to stress contingencies. Other European states fought wars, but without their representative institutions developing a role comparable to that of Parliament. It was in the seventeenth century, for reasons that were far from inevitable, that the Westminster Parliament diverged from the more general tendency towards a smaller, or even nonexistent, role for representative institutions. This divergence was due to political developments in Britain, to the failure of the Crown to secure an adequate resource base, and, critically, to the intervention of William of Orange in 1688, an intervention that ended James II's attempt to create a British absolutism on the French model.

Nationalism and Politicisation

The British civil wars of 1638–52 brought these and other issues to the fore and also, as civil wars abruptly do, demonstrated the problematic nature of national consciousness: it did not prevent a brutal domestic struggle. A national consciousness can be seen as an opposition to, or constraint on, a European awareness, but that is not too helpful an approach, as such an awareness was not particularly strong. Instead, it was more commonly the case of different national consciousnesses in competition.

In practice, states and 'peoples' are rarely united with shared views and a common purpose. However, national myths about present identity and past history generally pretend otherwise. As public politics, especially those associated with a culture of print and a representative system, led to a discourse of national consciousness, the need to define such a concept in an acceptable fashion increased. It was politicised, taken from the literary discourse of nationhood that had been characteristic of the later-medieval period, and given a number of competing partisan interpretations. This was readily apparent from the sixteenth century only, although it would be mistaken to underrate the extent and politicisation of national identity in the fifteenth century. However, such an identity increasingly meant, as a result of the Reformation, a number of different though overlapping and related national identities.

Presented as a consequence and source of unity, nationalism, or at least the language of national consciousness, was the product of division and was itself divisive. Indeed, it was as national divisions encompassing large numbers outside the élite became politically important that the language of national unity became politically significant. It was part of a process in which élite and non-élite political groups manoeuvred, united and were united in a common cause, one seeking more support. The language was also a defence against the disunity of political division.

The politicisation linked to the Reformation and to printing was not identical to the creation of national consciousness and could, indeed, be at cross-purposes to it, most obviously through an emphasis on confessional internationalism. The confessional struggle existed at every stage, from the individual conscience to the apocalyptic, but it was at the national level that the crucial political decisions were made about which faith was to be the established (official) one, and how the worship was to be organised. Similarly, issues of faith and ecclesiastical government, and contemporary hostility to notions of toleration, ensured that these decisions, once made, were to be implemented throughout the state. Indeed, distinctive religious arrangements became an expression and definition of state identity, an identity that was opposed to rival interpretations, both abroad and at home. In particular, the Reformation produced the vernacular Bible, and this Bible was the one that had to be used.

In England, the role of Parliament in articulating and encapsulating a sense of national identity and interest cannot be removed from the partisan context in which this was contested, but that very context helped to accentuate this role, especially in the seventeenth century. This was most particularly the case when the monarch could seem foreign. Such foreignness was in part a matter of the Scottish, Dutch and Hanoverian origins and interests of the monarchs after 1603, and also of their real and apparent religious views. Religion was crucial to national identity and to concerns about the monarch.

Nineteenth-century confidence in definitions of national interest relating to territorial consolidation and expansion, domestic order and stability, and national strength are of little help in the understanding of the mid- and later seventeenth century. Domestically, there was no constitutional, political or confessional consensus, and this lay behind the contentious politics of the period. Thus, popular post-Reformation ceremonies of identity and identification, such as Guy Fawkes celebrations, already discussed in one particular light as ceremonies of nationalism, were also occasions of contention between political and religious groups, at both the national and the local scales.

Thanks to the civil wars of 1638–52 and, even more, the Glorious Revolution of 1688–9 and its aftermath, both England

and Britain as a whole diverged from a more common pattern of European development. This parallel was understood by contemporaries. Had Charles I succeeded, then the Stuart monarchy could have been placed alongside those of the Bourbons and the Austrian Habsburgs. The defeat of the Crown in 1638–52, instead, led to new political, constitutional and ecclesiastical arrangements. However, the return of royal authority in 1660 with the restoration of Charles II (r. 1660–85) was seen by contemporaries as offering the possibility of a measure of convergence in the shape of British absolutism to emulate comparable Continental regimes.

This prospectus, which fired up critics of Charles, was ended by James II's failure in 1688–9. Stability was already challenged before the Glorious Revolution of those years. When James II (r. 1685–8), James VII of Scotland, moved away from any attempt to create or sustain a Protestant political consensus, there was a challenge to the hard-won stability eventually achieved under Charles II. Indeed, James's accession in 1685 was followed by domestic conspiracy, a foreign invasion arising from the Dutch marriage of James's elder (Protestant) daughter in 1677, dynastic coup and constitutional change, and, from 1689, by civil war in Scotland and Ireland.

Thus, Britain diverged from what was then a widespread European path of domestic stabilisation around the Crown. The nation-wide reconciliation between Crown and élites did not occur until the mid-eighteenth century, and then in very different circumstances from those on the Continent.

3

THE EIGHTEENTH CENTURY

From 1688, Britain might seem to have diverged from a common European course, and its politicians certainly thought it had. In part, this was because of a more 'liberal' constitutional regime created in the Revolution Settlement that followed the 'Glorious Revolution'. But this divergence from absolutism was also a result of other aspects of the breach in the succession in 1688, and the consequent instability and civil violence, much of which had religious as well as political aspects. These aspects included the relationship between the constituent parts of the British Isles. This, thus, represented a repetition, albeit with considerable differences, of the situation arising from the Henrician Reformation of the 1530s, and occurred at a time when, in contrast, domestic political and religious order had been restored in most European states. On the Continent, absolutism was a matter of this order, as much as of any constitutional formulations.

Such disorder was not, however, restricted to Britain in the early eighteenth century. The continued problems that the Habsburgs faced in Hungary, with a substantially Protestant nobility keen on its privileges and on limiting the powers of the

Habsburg sovereign, in the late seventeenth and early eighteenth century, culminated in the large-scale Rákóczi rebellion of 1703–11. This indicated the difficulties that a nobility with a sense of distinct political and religious privileges could create in the absence of harmony with the Crown. Royal power in Hungary was not to increase appreciably until the reigns of Charles VI (1711–40) and, more particularly, Maria Theresa (1740–80) brought a measure of such co-operation. In Spain, the long and bitter war of succession following the death of Charles II in 1700 did not have a religious aspect, but was related to the struggle for primacy between Castile and the lands of the Crown of Aragon, particularly Catalonia, a struggle that still resonates today.[1]

Britain cannot therefore be seen as truly unique in the challenge to governmental authority. In addition, albeit with the delays consequent upon the disruption of and from the 1680s, Britain took part in the more general movement towards a reconciliation between crowns and élites that was so characteristic of Europe in the late seventeenth century. In England and Wales, moreover, there was far less resistance than in Scotland and Ireland to William III and, after 1714, to the new Hanoverian dynasty. The extent of enthusiasm for them was limited. Nevertheless, Parliament and the government, both central and local, secular and ecclesiastical, were dominated by the nobility and their relatives and dependants, and this brought a measure of unity.

In England, the religious settlement of 1688–9, to which the exclusion of the Catholic James II (and VII) was central, an outcome confirmed with the Act of Settlement of 1701, ended several decades, indeed a century and a half, of uncertainty over the position of the Church of England. This outcome served as a basis for the development of new constitutional relationships between Crown and Parliament and, eventually, for a less volatile political situation. Politics were contentious, and the fundamental stability of the system was challenged by the Stuart claim to the throne, but, compared to the political world of 1678–88, that after 1689, especially after the consolidation of Whig hegemony in 1716–21, was more settled.

The situation, however, was less benign if Scotland and Ireland are included. The new order there was enforced in each at the cost of the exclusion of important sections both of the general population and of the élite. In addition to acute short-term disruption there was, especially in Ireland, a lasting sense of grievance.

Allowing for similarities between Britain and the Continent in terms of the move towards order, the Glorious Revolution led to a stronger contemporary emphasis on exceptionalism (the notion that the country was distinctive), which has been of considerable importance since in British thought. The Whig tradition made much of the redefinition of parliamentary monarchy in which Parliament met every year, of regular elections (as a result of the Triennial Act of 1694), of the freedom of the press (as a consequence of the lapsing of the Licensing Act in 1695), and of the establishment in 1694 of a funded national debt focused on the Bank of England. Each was a key element first in English and then in British exceptionalism.

The Revolution Settlement was seen by most British and many foreign commentators as clearly separating Britain from the general pattern of Continental development. Indeed, to use a modern term, it was as if history had ended, for, if history was an account of the process by which the constitution was established and defended, then the Revolution Settlement could be presented as a definitive constitutional settlement. It was argued that the Glorious Revolution had saved Britain from the general European move towards absolutism and a widespread move towards Catholicism. Not only people in Britain held these views. In Strasbourg in 1753, Voltaire told William Lee, a well-connected English tourist, that he (Lee) came from 'the only nation where the least shadow of liberty remains in Europe'. The following year, Stanisław Poniatowski, later king of Poland, visited England. His friendship with Charles Yorke, a prominent lawyer, would inspire his reforming constitutionalism as king.[2]

Britain was a European power and a world presence. From 1714 until 1837, the king was also Elector of Hanover. For much of the period 1689–1815, Britain was at war with other European powers. From 1689, she operated very much as part of the Continental political system. War and foreign policy contributed powerfully to the character of the British state. This state was less different from its counterparts on the Continent than is sometimes appreciated. After the protracted (and varied but interrelated) divisions of the period 1638–1716, there had been a re-creation of stable government by means of a new consensus. In this consensus, which incorporated much, but not all, of the political nation, patronage and the avoidance of radical changes were dominant, and thus the path of government was smoothed by practices that lessened the chance of unpredictable developments, practices, in short, that neutered political activity. Therefore, despite the role of a permanent and quite effective Parliament, the 'Old Corps' (ministerial) Whigs could be seen as having created, during the reigns of George I (r. 1714–27) and George II (r. 1727–60), a state that bore comparison with both strong Continental monarchies and with that attempted by the Stuarts.

Throughout Europe, the cosmopolitan aspects of eighteenth-century life and culture were matched by more parochial worlds, the two generally coexisting with little difficulty as they reflected the experiences and preoccupations of different social milieux. In Britain, the relationship was less easy because of a strong discourse, if not polemic, of cultural nationalism, which was a marked feature in sections of the world of print throughout the century.

This polemic was felt most urgently in London, a metropolitan forcing house of political, social and cultural tension. The vigorous xenophobia of London newspapers was matched by hostility to foreigners, most obviously in riots against French actors, as in 1738, 1739, 1743, 1749 and 1755. More generally, there is clear evidence of tension over cultural borrowing from the Continent, notably hostility towards being 'a ridiculous Ape of French Manners'. Criticism of this borrowing encompassed a certain amount of not so much class conflict, for a fully articulated class system did not exist, as social tension. A sense of cultural betrayal was brilliantly symbolised by food imagery, the claim that, in place of the 'roast beef of Old England', the aristocracy and the royal court preferred Continental food and, in particular, French cuisine, with its alleged insubstantiality: sauce not meat. Smuggling, notably of French brandy and silks, was another aspect of challenge and betrayal.

Much of the expression of xenophobia was clearly an aspect of propaganda by opposition groups, but such propaganda was only efficacious because it played on an established and accepted theme. Behind it can be discerned a sense of social betrayal and cultural fear: a sense that cosmopolitanism was a threat, both as a situation and as a tendency. It appeared to encapsulate unwelcome forces. Similarly, the homophobia of the period, with its emphasis on the alleged foreign (especially Italian) origin of sodomy, demonstrated an alliance between sexism and national chauvinism. Georges-Louis Lesage condemned the brutality and grossness of British manners, and, indeed, much of the foreign praise related to the nobility and the educated, not to the bulk of the population.[3] Foreign stereotypes of Englishness hardened without greatly changing even if most foreigners visited only southern England, particularly London.

One of the characteristic features of the British press was that it was a national press overwhelmingly printed in English. In contrast, French-language papers were distinctly marginal. Although foreign works were translated on a large scale for

English readers, foreign-language book and pamphlet publication in Britain was not common. The situation was very different across most of the Continent, where publication in a language different from that of the native population encouraged cosmopolitanism and its identification with the world of learning, opinion, politics and fashion. In that sense, the position in Britain prefigured the consequences of linguistic nationalism in other countries during the nineteenth century. The cultural nationalism of so much of British public culture offered a definite challenge to cosmopolitanism, and there is little sign that in doing so it challenged traditional beliefs. Far from the press expressing novel cultural attitudes, it was giving new force to the politico-cultural inheritance from the sixteenth and seventeenth centuries, especially anti-Catholicism and national self-sufficiency.

Eighteenth-Century England as the Model of a Progressive Society

For fashionable intellectuals on the Continent, however, Britain offered a model of a progressive society, one that replaced the Dutch model that had been so attractive the previous century, though there was also criticism of aspects of British society. The perception by Continental intellectuals was crucial to the presentation of Britain as a progressive society. Many eighteenth- and nineteenth-century French and German historians and lawyers looked to Britain as culturally and constitutionally superior, and thus as a model to be copied. They talked, however, about 'England' not 'Britain'. For Georg Christoph Lichtenberg (1742–99), the London of the 1770s was an exciting centre of civilisation where he could meet Priestley or Banks and see Garrick on the stage. British institutions were widely admired, and the most influential thinkers of the century included British philosophers and political economists.

Britain was not only praised by intellectuals from nearby states. Its impact was wider-ranging. Swedes who hoped to improve their political system looked to British constitutional practice, to trial by jury, primogeniture, independent local government and other features of British society. However, as later with the French revolutionaries, their analysis of the situation in Britain was sometimes overly simplistic, if not misleading, and there were aspects that they did not seek to emulate.

English literature was more widely read abroad than ever before, and, for the first time, Britain had a school of native painters, whose work merited comparison with the best in Europe. The young Johann Winckelmann, later an influential writer on cultural history, was influenced by *Cato's Letters*, a British opposition periodical that he read in the library of a Saxon aristocrat. Montesquieu, Voltaire and Rousseau, the leading French writers of the century, all visited England and were well acquainted with the leading figures of British intellectual life. More minor French figures also visited Britain, corresponded with British intellectuals, and read British books. Pierre-Joseph Alary, the founder of the Club de l'Entresol, an influential intellectual Parisian club of the 1720s which included the British ambassador Horatio Walpole among its members, spoke English and greatly enjoyed his trip to England in 1725. On it, he met Sir Isaac Newton and attended a meeting of the Royal Society, a popular venue for many French tourists. The British constitution was praised in the *Encyclopédie* (1751–65), initially a project to translate Ephraim Chambers's *Cyclopaedia or an Universal Dictionary of Arts and Sciences* (1728), although it was swiftly transformed into a vehicle for propaganda for the ideas of the *philosophes*, French thinkers who presented themselves as progressive and enlightened.

With time, Britain became more important as an economic model and a source of technological and entrepreneurial innovation. Duke Karl of Brunswick received details of a planned English lottery in 1740.[4] Foreign travellers reported on British manufacturing. British machinery, especially textile machinery, was smuggled abroad, and skilled British workers were recruited by foreign manufacturers. Crucial Continental manufacturing plants owed their origin to British skills. The Society of Arts in London had connections with most of the major economic societies on the Continent, and disseminated knowledge of British innovations.

Britain was also attractive as a financial proposition for investment. Foreign, particularly Dutch, holdings in the British national debt were significant, but they were only one aspect of the important financial and business links that bound Britain and the Continent, more especially London and Amsterdam, together. The Huguenot diaspora played a major role in this relationship, as did its Jewish counterpart, which was also important in Anglo-Portuguese financial relations.

Similarly, British and Irish families had members or connections abroad. Catholic Irish merchants had close links with Iberia and France, while English and Scottish merchants had many connections in the Low Countries. William III found titles for Dutch favourites—William Bentinck becoming Earl of Portland—while, under Anne, John Churchill, 1st Duke of Marlborough, was made a Prince of the Holy Roman Empire.

Continental intellectuals often neglected to note the fundamental controversies that were such an obvious feature of the Hanoverian period, or offered a simple account that found virtue only on one side, although there was criticism. In part this was a product of the influence of British opposition writers, especially Bolingbroke, although it also looked back to the seventeenth-century tradition of seeing Britain as inherently violent, a tradition that owed much to the English Civil War. In the eighteenth century, there was continued criticism of British political instability, partisanship and turbulence; but there was also an openness to British arguments about corruption, arguments that reflected what was seen, on the part of French conservatives offended by British society, as a long-standing obsession with property, trade and greed. Muralt attacked the role of corruption, while the *Encyclopédie* was not free from criticism. In his *Réflexions sur le gouvernement britannique*, Holbach castigated the corruption of British public life (for which he cited a British political pamphlet), the instability of British politics, and the venality, viciousness, arrogance and injustice of the British nation, although he also noted that, in the eyes of many, the British constitution was a major achievement of the human spirit.

Within Britain, politics, religion, culture and morality—none of them really separable—were occasions and sources of strife and polemic, and the same was true not only of views of recent history, most obviously the Revolution Settlement, but also of the very question of the relationship between Britain and the Continent. Alongside the notion of uniqueness as derived from and encapsulated in that Settlement, there was also a habit, especially marked in opposition circles, of seeking parallels abroad. These were designed to make polemical points, but their use also reflected a sense that parallels could be drawn. Thus, the long ministry of Sweden's Count Horn could be compared with that of Walpole, while the opposition press could suggest in 1732–3 that the Parlement of Paris was readier to display independence than the Westminster Parliament.[5]

This habit was accentuated from 1714 by the Hanoverian connection, for, under both George I and George II, the contentiousness of that connection led to a sustained political discourse about the extent to which Britain was both being ruled in accordance with the foreign interests of her monarchs and being affected in other ways, especially cultural. A London item in the *Bristol Gazette and Public Advertiser* of 12 September 1771 argued the case for similarities between British and French developments:

There is a striking similitude between the present situation of the people of England and the people of France. In both the people are alike oppressed; in both the finances of the public are in a wretched condition; in both the reins of government are guided by a woman; in both their Parliaments have been essentially suppressed, the one by force, the other by fraud; in both their Princes do not rely on the affections of their subjects, but on large standing armies; in both the King's will and pleasure is the only law; in both the just and consti-tutional rights and liberties of the people have been infringed and trampled upon; in both there have been frequent remonstrances to their kings, which have been totally disregarded; and in both there is such a general ferment and discontent, they may probably bring on a confusion, and end in a change of their present forms of conduct.

If the frequently reiterated view of France as a menacing despo-tism heavily influenced British public debate, it did not preclude praise for specific aspects of French society and government. On 25 June 1737, the prohibition of slaughtering meat in Paris was held up for emulation in *Wye's Letter*, the leading London manu-script newsletter, and French regulatory practices were frequently applauded. Indeed, citing French examples in a hostile fashion could lead to disputes. When a ministerial speaker claimed in the House of Commons in 1717 that French taxes were as heavy as those in Britain and their collecting methods more grievous, an opposition MP retorted that French manufacturing and com-merce were increasing, an approach that reflected a sense of threat. On 17 February 1722, *Applebee's Original Weekly Journal*, a London newspaper, challenged one of the fundamental premises of British political thought when it cited France as an example for attacking the claim in the *London Journal* that trade required liberty. In 1736, in a debate in the Lords on a bill to prevent smuggling, it was claimed that, despite punitive legal powers in France, smuggling there was nearly as bad as in Britain. Sir Robert Walpole observed in the Commons in 1739:

gentlemen, in their opposition to the administration, make it their business to collect precedents and examples from our neighbours, and if they can find anything parallel to them practised by the government, let it be never so reasonable, then it is always the universal clamour that the government immediately designs to reduce the whole constitution to the French form, that they make themselves arbitrary. But if some gentlemen have a favourite measure in view which corresponds with anything practised by the French government, that agreement is so far from being a reproach to it, and a reason why it ought not to be pursued that it is recommended solely on that account.[6]

Walpole was more correct in his first point. However, this range of reference indicates the problems with modern judgements that simplify attitudes, and also throws light on the difficulties in assessing the degree of similarity or contrast between Britain and Continental states in this period.

Eighteenth-century British, particularly English, political debates looked back to the controversies of the previous century over Gothicism and the Norman Yoke. These centred on the notion that post-Roman Europe was originally unified by sharing Germanic freedoms, but that this liberty of the forest had been lost in England as a consequence of William I's victory in 1066 and the imposition of the Norman Yoke, an argument that had been pushed by opponents of the Stuarts and was inherited by the Whigs. Thus, England needed to restore its original freedom, a freedom that it had shared with the Continent, but that had been lost. This loss was seen as being the result in England of invasion and, across much of Europe, of political developments and, in particular, the corrupting tendencies of the medieval Church, itself a corruption of the primitive Church. The Glorious Revolution could be presented as a recovery of original freedoms, a process that separated Britain from most of Continental Europe.

A shared heritage, nevertheless, could reflect differences in literary and political culture as different elements in that heritage were highlighted. This was true, for example, of the very important Classical heritage. Thus, in England the French were seen as fawning followers of Horace, civilised, urbane, sophisticated, fashionable servants or slaves; the English as rugged, no-nonsense, plain-speaking followers of Juvenal, hence free. The glory of Augustan Rome encompassed both Horace and Juvenal, but in England and Scotland there was an important theme of Classical republican virtue that looked back to republican Rome. This has been termed the 'Catonic perspective', a reference to an image of Cato that was powerful in the early eighteenth century.[7]

While the modern political notion of British specificity and uniqueness dates from the Glorious Revolution, its economic counterpart is dated later and less specifically, from the second half of the eighteenth century. However, the Industrial Revolution can in part be linked to the earlier political changes by arguing that they were a crucial prerequisite (for example, by offering security against the fiscal policies of an arbitrary government), an argument that by its very nature is difficult to prove or disprove. Moreover, it is possible to emphasise an earlier and longer-term genesis for industrialisation. As with the Glorious Revolution, the very nature and consequences of the Industrial Revolution are matters of serious historical dispute. The Hanoverian age has been returned to the context of fundamental controversy, which was such an obvious feature of the period.

The Glorious Revolution was crucial to the Whig myth, or interpretation of British history, and central to the notion of British uniqueness. Celebrating the centenary, the *Leeds Mercury* of 11 November 1788 declared that 'It was from that glorious period, [that] the animating breath of Liberty has diffused peace and increased commerce among the subjects of Britain'. Political and religious liberty were seen as mutually supportive. In the dedication of 1760 for the fourteenth edition of his *A New History of England*, the prolific writer John Lockman (1698–1771) 'endeavoured to set the whole in such a light, as may inspire the readers with an ardent love for our pure religion, and its darling attendant, liberty; and, on the other hand, with a just abhorrence of popery, and its companion, slavery'.[8] Lockman was one of the large number of mostly overlooked lesser writers on numerous topics who helped to reiterate public ideology. In 1760, he published *A History of the Cruel Sufferings of the Protestants and Others by Popish Persecutions in Various Countries*. As secretary to the British Herring Fishery, Lockman sought to develop the industry in the Shetlands.

A sense of being outside Europe characterised most British political debate. It strengthened and intertwined with other senses of uniqueness or specificity that were not without cause. The common law was seen as a particularly English creation, was contrasted with legal precepts and practice in, above all, France, and enjoyed marked attention in the age of the jurist Sir William Blackstone (1723–80). Indeed, Blackstonian notions of the constitution as an appropriately regulated system of checks and balances played a major role in the ideology of the late-eighteenth-century British state.

The British social system was praised for its lack of social distinctions and its degree of social mobility, and for the presence, in both town and countryside, of intermediate groups that enjoyed a measure of prosperity and position. Thus, in 1792, John Trevor, the long-serving Envoy Extraordinary in Turin, reported,

> the misfortune is that in this country [Kingdom of Sardinia, more particularly Piedmont] the whole society is divided into two classes, the *Court* and *Nobility*, and the *Bourgeoisie*, and the line drawn between them is so rude and marked that the two Parties have long been jealous and might too easily become *hostile*; there are none of

those intermediate shades which blend the whole together into one harmonious mass as in our happy country.[9]

Aspects of the British situation conducive to social cohesion, such as social mobility, have been cited as a major reason why Britain avoided revolution in the 1790s, although so did other European states, such as Russia, whose social circumstances were somewhat different.

Views of foreign countries were an important means by which attitudes to British government and society were advanced and debated. France dominated Britain's conceptions of the outside world, and negative themes prevailed. France was generally presented as an autocracy and a society run by a corrupt and effete court, which, simultaneously, used violence to maintain its position—the Bastille, *lettres de cachet* and torture—and yet did not need to do so because the populace were happy: their faculties ensnared by Catholicism, and their past liberties surrendered thanks to corruption. Historical arguments were based on the view that national character, far from being immutable, could alter as a result of social and political changes—a warning to Britain. In 1740, George Lyttelton, an opposition Whig MP, declared in the Commons: 'It is not Spanish or French arms, but Spanish and French maxims of government that we should have most to fear.'[10]

The public myth of uniqueness that played such a major role in the Whig inheritance (by the 1760s most politicians could see themselves as Whigs) was qualified, from 1688 on, by domestic critics who charged, with reason, that the Whigs had abandoned their late-seventeenth-century radical ideas, and who also sometimes denied that the British system was better than those across the Channel. Particular attention was focused on the way in which the 'executive' had allegedly subverted the freedom of Parliament by corruption. In short, the Revolution Settlement could be subverted from within, by moral and political corruption, the two aspects of the same threat, continually challenging the achievement of liberty, so that the price of liberty was eternal vigilance. This was a view particularly associated, in the first half of the eighteenth century, with the Opposition Whigs, critical of the governing 'Old Corps' Whigs, and with Hanoverian Tories, willing to work with George I and George II but unhappy about government policy. Though different in their analysis and political prescription, those who held these views could still agree that the Revolution Settlement was distinctive and worth preserving, and this was the assessment picked up and propagated by foreign communicators. Critics of this assessment of the Revolution Settlement existed, but both the Jacobites and the radical Whigs, who criticised all or many aspects of the post-1688 world, had been marginalised by military and political developments.

However, comparisons with Continental monarchy were to be pressed home in the 1760s and early 1770s when George III (1760–1820) broke with the tutelage of the 'Old Corps' Whigs and found himself accused of hankering for absolute monarchy. Contemporaries searched for parallels in the Maupeou Revolution in France (1771) and in Gustavus III's coup in Sweden (1772), both of which were seen as measures designed to subordinate 'intermediate institutions' to Crown authority, and in the Swedish case as a *coup d'état* for the monarchy. Nevertheless, at the same time, many British politicians made comparisons between Britain and Sweden after 1772 to the latter's disadvantage. French views of the British political system became more critical from the 1760s in response to the controversy within Britain over the intentions of George III. This culminated in widespread fashionable support across Europe for the American revolutionaries.

Cultural Links

Aside from close political links, there were important cultural relations between Britain and the Continent, both continuing and developing ones. In the eighteenth century, the British élite was culturally very attuned to Continental developments. This was linked to a degree of cosmopolitanism in British intellectual life, as shown for example, from the 1760s, by the quest for impartiality by prominent historians such as Edward Gibbon and William Robertson, both of whom were European figures.

The royal court was less important as a source and sphere of cultural patronage than was the case in most Continental states, although it did serve, under William III, George I and George II, as a means for the dissemination of Continental artistic developments. George I was an active patron of the German-born composer Georg Friedrich Handel, who was naturalised in 1726, George II of the German enamellist C.F. Zincke. The sea therefore proved no barrier to foreign influences.

William III's arrival from Holland in 1688, and the coming of George I from Hanover in 1714, imposed Calvinist and Lutheran monarchs, and opened the way to Dutch and Germans who followed in their wake. In the same decades, persecutions on the Continent introduced other adherents of foreign churches. Refugees from France and the Catholic parts of the Holy Roman Empire—Huguenots, Palatines and Moravians—sought sanctuary in London, but resisted integration into the English establishment and worshipped separately from their new hosts, although by the mid-eighteenth century the Huguenots conformed, largely through Archbishop Secker's influence. He encouraged the French congregations in London and Southampton to conform to Anglican liturgy translated into French. More significantly, the Huguenot diaspora helped to consolidate and broaden intellectual and cultural relations, not least in furthering the important Holland–London news axis of the early British press. Indeed, the international republic of letters had important British branches.

A network of correspondents and lobbyists introduced foreign ideas and works into Britain, including forms of foreign spirituality. A prime example was the fascination with the Pietist experiment at Halle. The educational and social work undertaken by these German Protestants became the inspiration for many British initiatives, gaining particular converts among enthusiasts for workhouses, charity schools and the SPCK.

Furthermore, the already strong appeal of Continental Catholic culture to part of the British élite, which had been such an obvious feature of the courts of Charles I and Charles II, became more marked in the early eighteenth century. This was not due to religion but to the vogue for the Grand Tour and the consequent personal influence on prominent individuals. Cultural, stylistic, intellectual and religious fashions and impulses crossed the Channel and had a major impact on the British élite, as well as an influence on other groups. They included Italian opera, Palladianism, French cooking, card games and pornography, the Rococo, Neoclassicism, Protestant evangelicalism, and, in the 1780s, ballooning. The morning levée was introduced into Britain from France, as was the umbrella.

A large number of French artists practised in Britain, particularly from the 1710s to 1760s, the period of Rococo influences. Alexandre Desportes painted many hunting scenes on his visit in 1712–13. Maurice Quentin de La Tour, a portrait painter admired by Hogarth, had a successful visit to London in 1723. Andien de Clermont spent the mid-1710s to the mid-1750s in England, carrying out decorative painting at Kew, Strawberry Hill and Wilton. The portrait painter Jean van Loo arrived in London in 1737 and spent a lucrative five years taking commissions from resentful English rivals. The draughtsman Hubert Gravelot arrived in London in 1733 and stayed until the 1745 Jacobite rebellion led him and his compatriot, the artist Philip Mercier, to leave for France. As a teacher at the St Martin's Lane Academy, Gravelot trained a whole generation of British artists, including Gainsborough. The painter Charles Clérisseau was invited to London in 1771 by Robert Adam and exhibited with much success at the Royal Academy. Italian, Swiss and German artists were also important: Canaletto, Zuccarelli, Cipriani, Kauffmann and Zoffany.

British porcelain was influenced by French models, as were other crafts. The role of French society as a model for genteel behaviour was significant in the importance of French dancing masters, hairdressers and clothes-makers. Moreover, the ready availability of translations played a significant role in cultural interchange. Translations ranged from the works of Pope and Shakespeare to Robert Chasles's amorous scandalous fiction which appeared in its first English edition in 1727 (a second following twelve years later) as *The Illustrious French Lovers; being the histories of the amours of several French persons of quality*. More utility might have been derived from the 1757 first French edition of John Bartlet's veterinary work or from *A Treatise upon the Culture of Peach Trees* (1768), a translation of Combles's 1745 book.

The works of some leading Continental intellectuals were influential in Britain. This was particularly true of Montesquieu and the Italian legal writer Beccaria. Montesquieu's major work, *L'Esprit des loix* (1748), was published in a translation by Thomas Nugent two years later. Born in Ireland, Nugent spent most of his life in London, and his work as a translator indicated the close interest shown in Britain in intellectual developments on the Continent. His translations included Jean-Baptiste Dubos's *Critical Reflections on Poetry, Painting, and Music* (1748), Burlamaqui's *Principles of Natural Law* (1748) and his *Principles of Politic Law* (1752), Voltaire's *Essay on Universal History* (1759), and Rousseau's *Emilius* (1763). Nugent also published accounts of his travels on the Continent, a history of Mecklenburg, whence George III's wife, Queen Charlotte, had come, and an English–French pocket dictionary.

The popularity of such dictionaries was a testimony to the strength of foreign cultural links, as well as a product of the rise in book ownership. More direct influences can be seen in the works of some writers. Stephen Payne Adye, the Deputy Judge Advocate, acknowledged his debt to Montesquieu and Beccaria in his *Essay on Military Punishments and Rewards* (1769), which called for the enlightened reform of the British system of military justice. The willingness of some commentators to look at Continental ideas and models is notable given the distinctive character of the English legal system. A laudatory tone characterised the well-travelled William Mildmay's *The Police of France: or, An Account of the Laws and Regulations Established in the Kingdom for the Preservation of Police and the Preventing of Robberies* (1763). Moreover, there was increased knowledge of Europe due to the publication of books about geography and the use of geographical material in the press.[11]

The direction of influence was not all one way: English landscaping had a major impact abroad, as in the grounds of the king of Naples' new palace at Caserta. Yet, landscaping was adopted more readily because it was partly modelled on a truly cosmopolitan source, the Classics. More generally, British influence abroad was strong in intellectual life and literature. Freemasonry spread from Britain into fashionable Continental circles. Modern authors, such as the novelists Henry Fielding and Laurence Sterne and the philosopher Anthony, 3rd Earl of Shaftesbury, and earlier writers, in particular Shakespeare, had a considerable impact in the Low Countries and Germany. Ossian, the Scottish Homer, swept Europe, and, translated into several European languages, including German (1768), French (1777), Russian (1792), Dutch (1805), Danish (1807–9) and Czech (1827), influenced Goethe, Napoleon and Schiller. The appearance of a translation of Ossian played a crucial role in the plot of Goethe's *Werther* (1774). Other British works were not self-consciously primitive. In Russia, in 1741–1800, 245 books were published that can be traced back to original English-language works by

British authors, many via a French translation. The Russian dramatist Alexander Sumarokov first produced his adaptation of *Hamlet* in 1750, although the anguish of the original was replaced by clear moral purpose. Cultural links stemmed from an interest in foreign countries that encouraged comparison.

National Distinctiveness

It is also instructive to look for comparisons in more modern terms. These can be anachronistic, but also fruitful. In employing criteria, there is often a search for functional, rather than ideological, structures, that is on how systems worked, rather than on the values they affirmed. One such structure was that of multiple statehood, a characteristic Britain shared with, for example, Austria, Prussia, Spain and Denmark. In other words, it was an amalgamation of formerly disparate units that at least in part retained a separate governmental identity. At the same time, such states had a centre of activity. The crushing of the 1745 Jacobite rising in the battle of Culloden in 1746 both encouraged a new burst of British trans-oceanic imperialism,[12] and ensured that the new British state created by the parliamentary union of England and Scotland in 1707 would continue to be one whose political tone and agenda were set in London and southern England.

This was the basis of British consciousness, a development that did not so much alter the views of the English political élite, for whom Britain was essentially an extension of England, but, rather, reflected the determination of the Scottish and, to a lesser extent, Welsh and Irish Protestant élites to link their fate with that of the British state; indeed, the Anglican élite in Ireland persisted in defining itself as English (although this was changing fast from the 1760s).

Much that was already in existence was confirmed and strengthened by the Revolution Settlement and the Act of

Union, and much that was the product of the politics of the surrounding decades seems familiar now. By 1707, the ideas of limited government, an accountable monarchy, the role of law, and an absence of religious persecution (if Catholics would not have agreed, they were far better treated than Protestant counterparts in Catholic Europe) were being clearly established as aspects of the Revolution Settlement.

They have all been part of Britain's 'deep history' ever since. As well as having great constitutional and political force, the legal and political practices affirmed and created also reflected and sustained assumptions, notably a belief in fairness and accountability, that could be handed down to new generations and to immigrants. Since 1689 and 1707, these assumptions have provided a historical basis for a democratic culture in British history, one that is not simply grounded in constitutional provisions. Indeed, modern British democratic culture reflects a pervasive historicism in the form of values grounded in past events and practice.

Such a development did not, however, prevent the coincident, still vigorous senses of local, provincial and national identities. This situation repeated the earlier combination of the English national myth with the linguistic, cultural and ethnic diversity of an England that stretched from Cornwall, whose distinctive language only disappeared in about 1780, to the Scottish borders. As so often, such combinations were in part expressed through hostility to outsiders. This process of nationalism was not unique to Britain but was shared by Continental societies, albeit also within the context of multiple identities and with a cultural rather than a political focus.

Yet, the continued, indeed (from 1694 and 1707) greater role of the Westminster Parliament was a major difference from the situation in most of Europe, and was seen as such both in Britain and on the Continent. In Parliament, Britain had a more effective 'hinge' or means of obtaining, eliciting, sustaining and legitimating co-operation between the Crown and a widespread political nation for the achievement of common action than existed in other European states of comparable size. After 1688 institutions and, more importantly, a political culture embodying genuine modes of representation had developed in Britain. This process helped give a distinctive character to British politics and led foreign visitors to show particular interest in attending both parliamentary debates and elections. The sight of a first minister having to defend policy was not a familiar one, and Prime Minister's Questions continues to fascinate foreign observers, American and Continental.

The scrutiny of differences between Britain and the Continent has to make allowance for variations within the latter and must not be blind to those who suffered hardship within the British system. These included not only many in the British Isles but also others in the British world. Britain was the world's leading slave trader. Nevertheless, instructive contrasts can still be found. Although the Royal Navy continued to be dependent in wartime on forcible impressment by press gangs, there was no national system of conscription for land or sea service. Widespread conscription for the army on the model of Austria, Prussia, Sweden or Russia was unacceptable. Indeed, the very fact that Continental states resorted to such methods established them as unacceptable, although there was impressment of the unemployed during some periods of acute manpower shortage, for example during the War of the Spanish Succession. In 1756, a Press Act made possible the compulsory enlistment of 'such able-bodied men as do not follow any lawful calling or employment, or have not some other lawful and sufficient support and maintenance'. The Act, however, disappointed expectations. It proved difficult for officials to raise sufficient men, their quality was low, and desertion was a major problem. The system fell into disuse in 1758.

Britain lacked a regulatory regime and social system akin to that of Prussia or Russia, and, without them, it was difficult to make a success of conscription or to limit desertion. The army remained a volunteer force, and Britain remained unusual as a great power in that it did not have a large army. Including the Irish establishment, the peacetime army was only about 30,000 strong in the first half of the century, and 45,000 strong in the 1760s.

Furthermore, Britain's economic expansion, which was impressive by Continental standards, had an impact: job opportunities affected army recruitment, and recruitment for the navy was hit by the higher rates of pay provided by the merchant marine. The impact of commerce can also be seen in the use of subsidised foreign forces, for example Hessians and Dutch. It has been argued that the availability of such troops enabled Britain to have a freer use of its own labour and to preserve better its own liberties, but that this was achieved at the cost of an opposite process occurring in Hesse-Cassel.[13] This thesis, a variation on the core–periphery model of early to modern economic developments, with the periphery serving the needs of the core, offers an approach to the distinctive spatial and dynamic character of British power, as well as a way both to integrate Britain and the wider world and to look at relations within Britain. It can, for example, be extended to include the extensive recruitment of sepoys for the East India Company and also Scottish Highlanders for the British army from the mid-eighteenth century and, in the economic sphere, it helps to explain the use of slaves. At the same time, Britain was scarcely alone in these processes.

The apparent degree of difference between Britain and the Continent was eroded in the late eighteenth century by the widespread process of public politicisation on the Continent. In France this led to, and to a greater extent was first stimulated by, the mid-century controversies centring on Jansenism and later those arising from the Maupeou Revolution. Hence, by the

1780s, there was a considerable measure of convergence between aspects of the public politics of Britain and France.

In the 1770s and 1780s, French ministries sought to create a consensus similar to that offered by the British Parliament and to ground French government in institutions that were representative of public opinion, by planning provincial assemblies and then summoning first an Assembly of Notables (1787) and subsequently the Estates General (1789). Had the French succeeded in a programme of peaceful constitutional reform, then it would be possible to emphasise a degree of convergence with Britain. Initially, that indeed was the theme of supportive British commentators who, in 1789, enthusiastically noted the opening stages of what appeared to be a popular and successful revolution that could be compared with the events of 1688–9 in Britain.

Alongside political contrasts and similarities, however, there was a growing economic divergence between Britain and the Continent. In part, this reflected a more liberal economic and social structure and practice. The legal situation was linked to economic development. Because English law emphasised absolute ownership in right, the right to dispose of property as thought appropriate at death, and the landowner's right to minerals and coal under his property, it promoted enterprise and ensured that landlords were better placed to mobilise capital. Legal rights were important to English success in creating a transportation system that facilitated the emergence of new industries, regional specialisation, an increase in the scale and standardisation of production, and wider markets. In addition, the political institutions and culture of England were more conducive to the local initiatives and control required for the creation of new transportation links, the canals and turnpikes that proved crucial economic multipliers. In France, in contrast, control was more in the hands of a small bureaucracy that was less responsive to local needs, although in France the right to charge tolls, such as those on British turnpikes, was usually presented by reformers as an obstacle to wealth creation. The situation in England was eased by the possibility of establishing trusts by private Acts of Parliament, legislation that was an important function of Parliament, while in France the insistence on central government control precluded necessary private investment and led to a concentration on a small number of prestige projects.[14]

The use of resources was more generally significant. This was especially so in the case of coal. Britain had a long-standing rise in coal production during the seventeenth and eighteenth centuries, and coal both replaced wood as fuel and spawned a range of industries. Moreover, rising average real incomes provided an important pull on economic development and specialisation. In contrast, wood remained dominant over most of the Continent.[15] Innovation in Britain rested on a culture of scientific experimentation that drew on the competitive market for ideas.[16]

This provided Britain with a contrast to the situation not only on the Continent but also beyond it. Thus, the application of engineering knowledge in Britain reflected an understanding and use of Newtonian mechanics which represented considerable social capital and intellectual application that was lacking elsewhere in the world. Information was transmitted by example, publication and purchase, the viewing of steam engines in operation being an important means to this transmission, and one that became fashionable. Aside from advertising lectures and demonstrations, providing a market for the popular touring lecturers on Newton, British newspapers covered science as a topic. Scientific culture was widely diffused. Mid-century Northampton had a population of only about 5,000, but from 1743 to about 1751 it supported the Northampton Philosophical Society, whose lectures covered the full syllabus of contemporary physics.

In Britain, there was tension in the relationship between religion and science, but it was essentially positive. Scientific knowledge was presented as demonstrating God's laws, leading to social progress and moral reform. To an extent that was unusual, both the governmental and commercial contexts of cultural activity were characterised by a developing interest in change. That was easier in Britain due to the experience of re-moulding state and church in the aftermath of the Glorious Revolution. The idea that change could and should be planned, moulded and advanced was acceptable. Conversely, other societies were increasingly presented as backward because unchanging, a view the British particularly took of Spain. It was entirely in accordance with British self-interest that Britain beat France to discover, with John Harrison's chronometer, a reliable and predictable method for determining longitude at sea.

War and Identity

Britain emerges as distinctive because it was better able to develop and use dynamic relationships: trade, finance and force helped to structure relationships within the expanding Western world to Britain's benefit.[17] For example, the Royal Navy protected trade revenues that could finance subsidy forces. It would be misleading to contrast Britain and the Continent too starkly in this respect. Other Atlantic states sought to do the same, but the British system was supported by a more flexible practice of state regulation and was more open to entrepreneurial activity than those of the other two leading naval powers, France and Spain. Yet, British successes had to be fought for and then defended. For most of the period, Britain was at war with other European states (1689–97, 1702–13, 1718–20, 1739–48, 1754–63, 1778–83) or close to war (1725–9, 1733–5, 1770–1, 1776–7).

These conflicts exposed major differences in British politics and public opinion, notably between the two parties. The Whigs focused on grand European alliances and calls for international intervention while the Tory emphasis was on insularity, maritime power, an aversion to Continental commitments, and scepticism about external projects that impaired Britain's freedom of manoeuvre. These views were linked to the Tory concern about an over-expanded and expensive state, as well as avoidance of the burden of taxation necessary to maintain a large army and Continental commitments. Daniel Finch, 2nd Earl of Nottingham, a Tory Secretary of State from 1689 to 1693 and in 1702–4, was particularly significant in that he encouraged the development of 'blue water' policies. This distinctive strategy focused on maritime control and amphibious operations and contrasted with the commitment, on the part of William III and those close to him, to army operations in the Low Countries. Nottingham's contribution was taken forward during the 1710–14 Tory ministry by its leading ministers, Robert Harley, Earl of Oxford and Henry, Viscount Bolingbroke.

This contrast, one stronger in rhetoric than practice, but still important, helped ensure that debate over foreign policy was significant to the definition of British politics, and to a degree greater than was generally the case in Britain in preceding decades. This debate was not really resolved until the 1760s when successive ministries, while willing to seek alliances on the Continent, were nevertheless unwilling to become committed to its power politics to the extent seen under George I and George II. This shift reflected high-political changes but also drew on a popular disinclination to repeat the high-cost policies of those reigns.

The position in Britain thus altered under George III (r. 1760–1820), and for both political and cultural reasons. George never visited Hanover and took care to associate himself with Britain to a degree that both his predecessors had conspicuously neglected. Until the Fürstenbund (League of Princes) of 1785, in which George took a contentious role as Elector of Hanover, Hanoverian issues played little role in British foreign policy. Indeed, more generally, there was a shift from concern with Continental affairs to a political and governmental agenda dominated by domestic and imperial issues, a process that culminated in the War of American Independence (1775–83). Victory in the Seven Years War (1756–63) had left Britain as the world's leading naval power, and this had brought her extensive colonial gains: Canada, Senegal, Grenada, Tobago, Dominica, St Vincent, Florida. Culturally, there was more self-confidence and less concern about cultural borrowing. The Royal Academy, founded in 1768, and its long-serving first president, Sir Joshua Reynolds, advanced the dignity of British art.

The British view of the Continent in the 1760s, 1770s and 1780s was more distant than it had been over the previous century, but also less hostile. This can be seen in the move away from an often hostile Whiggish approach to foreign countries on the part of travellers, to a more varied response. Among the élite, hostility to Catholicism diminished. Catholics had maintained their own religious, cultural, educational and social links with the Continent, and in the late eighteenth century, as attitudes towards Catholicism became less hostile, they found this a less difficult process. Popular hostility to Catholicism, however, remained strong, as the Scottish agitation of 1778–82 against a proposal for Catholic relief, and the Gordon Riots of 1780 in England, most prominently London, both amply demonstrated.

Moreover, Britain's destiny after the Seven Years War increasingly appeared to be a matter of trans-oceanic interests, a process encouraged by the ultimately insoluble issues involved in seeking to manage the North American colonies. Thus, in the 1760s–1780s, there was a prefiguring of the 'interest, but no commitment' stance towards the Continent that was to define British policy for most of the century from 1815. William Pitt the Younger's determination in 1792 to avoid war with Revolutionary France was an aspect of this policy. Events, however, in the shape of the unexpected success of the Revolutionary forces, were to provoke a crisis that led in a different direction.

4

THE LONG NINETEENTH CENTURY

Whatever may be the course of circumstances, my political creed turns on the expediency of avoiding wars abroad and innovations at home: nothing else is wanting to confirm for a long period the elevated point on which we stand above all the nations of the world either in present times or in history.

A self-contained and somewhat distant political attitude towards the Continent was advocated by the MP and experienced diplomat William, Lord Auckland, who wrote to the Prime Minister, William Pitt the Younger, in February 1790. It was not to be. British policy changed dramatically as a result of the French Revolution. Although many of the revolutionaries looked to British institutions for inspiration, and Britain did not join Austria and Prussia in attacking Revolutionary France in 1792, war with France broke out the following February. With two brief gaps, it lasted until 1815.

Britain and the Challenge of the French Revolution

The French Revolution both accentuated and then ruptured the convergence between aspects of the public politics of Britain and

France that had been noticeable in the second half of the century. The French Estates General, which had last met in 1614, was not so much revived in 1789 as created anew, and this forum of national politics developed rapidly into a body before which, in comparison with Britain, the government was crippled. In France political, rather than institutional, reform came to the fore, despite the effort of the royal government to centre on the latter. The pace of this political reform, the urgent desire to create a new constitution, and, crucially, the opposition of powerful domestic elements to the process of reform and bitter divisions among those who sought change ensured that it soon became better described as revolution, both by its supporters and by its opponents. There was no time to establish widely acceptable constitutional conventions and the élite was fatally fractured.

As a result of the revolutionary crisis, a similar process occurred in Britain and in France in the early 1790s: the definition of a political perspective in which foreign and domestic challenges were closely linked, and in which it seemed crucial to mobilise mass support for a struggle with an insidious but also all too apparent enemy: an obvious foreign rival supporting domestic conspiracy and insurrection—a singularly modern theme. A language of nationalism, to which paranoia contributed, therefore developed. In France, however, revolution was the cause and consequence of this process of struggle, whereas in Britain the challenge of domestic radicalism and Revolutionary France led to a widespread rallying to Country, Crown and Church. This paralleled similar movements elsewhere in Europe.

Britain was also involved more closely with the Continent thanks to her major role in the struggle with Revolutionary, and then Napoleonic, France. This process culminated in the leading roles taken by Britain at the Congress of Vienna (1814–15) and on the battlefield of Waterloo (1815). The Revolution thus both focused British political concern on the Continent and introduced a marked ideological slant to British political culture, one in which domestic cultural and political preferences were clearly matched to, and given opposing force by, differing responses to the situation on the Continent.

The political shift was readily apparent. In 1739, Britain had gone to war with Spain as a consequence of competing views over Caribbean trade and, the following year, James Thomson composed 'Rule, Britannia' with its maritime theme:

Rule, Britannia, rule the waves
Britons never will be slaves.

In 1754, hostilities had begun with France over control of the Ohio River basin in North America. In 1778 Britain had gone to war with France as a result of Louis XVI's support for the American revolutionaries. Similarly, in 1770 Britain had nearly gone to war with the Bourbon powers (France and Spain) over the Falkland Islands, and in 1790 over Nootka Sound. Yet, in 1793, Britain began her longest period of continuous warfare since the Elizabethan war with Spain, not over the fate of empire, but over the control of the United Provinces. Indeed, in imperial terms there was no reason to go to war with Revolutionary France. France's navy was in a poor state and her energies were devoted to a Continental war for survival. The Continental focus of Britain's foreign policy was rarely so clear as in her repeated attempts to limit French power in 1793–1815.

These attempts had considerable impact on Britain, irrespective of the ideological challenge of revolution. British society was mobilised for war, not on a scale to compare with Revolutionary France, still less with modern 'total war', but, nevertheless, to an extent that was far greater than in other conflicts of the time. The unprecedented strains on public finance led to income tax, which was introduced as a wartime measure. The revived role of political economy produced the first national census. The country was mapped by the Ordnance Survey. In his essay 'Of Publick Debts', printed in his *Inquiry into the Nature and Causes of the Wealth of Nations* (1776), Adam Smith had claimed:

> In great empires the people who live in the capital, and in provinces remote from the scene of action, feel many of them scarce any inconveniency from the war; but enjoy, at their ease, the amusement of reading in the newspapers the exploits of their own fleets and armies. To them this amusement compensates the small difference between the taxes which they pay on account of the war, and those which they had been accustomed to pay in time of peace.

Such an interpretation might seem to be given literary backing by the world depicted in the novels of Jane Austen, but it is not one that a close reading of the period would support. The precarious world of credit and debt in which many urban artisans were trapped was dependent on international developments. The urban economy relied on trade, while its rural counterpart was affected by high taxation. Privateering, impressment and recruitment affected the national economy and bore down upon the economies of individual families.

Irrespective of their ideological position, the fate of the Continent therefore engaged the attention of the British during the Revolutionary and Napoleonic Wars; indeed, more so than in preceding wars of the period. After 1741 French advances into central Europe during the War of the Austrian Succession (1740–8) had been held and they had taken several years to conquer the Austrian Netherlands (Belgium); in the Seven Years War, the French had been less than successful in their German operations; and, in the War of American Independence, there had been no campaigns on the Continent, except for the unsuccessful siege of Gibraltar.

In contrast, the French overran much of Europe in the years from 1792, their rapid conquest of the whole of Belgium in November 1792 being but the first of their dramatic advances.

The frontiers of Italy, the Rhineland and the Low Countries had been stable for the half-century after 1748; now Europe was being remoulded, new political spaces being created, frontiers redrawn, all in the interests of France. The auxiliary republics of the 1790s became the ancillary kingdoms of the 1800s. France became an empire; the Holy Roman Empire came to an end. Neutrality and non-intervention was not apparently a plausible policy for Britain, no more than a lack of concern and interest was sensible for the British. Whether with the French intervention in Ireland in 1798 or with the Continental System—the Napoleonic attempt of 1806–13 to exclude British trade from the Continent—it was clear that French power affected many aspects of British life.

The ideological challenge was also a potent one that obliged commentators to rethink the nature of Britain's relations with the Continent. A combination of the potential universal mission of the new Republic, the real or feared aspirations of British radicals, and the response of British conservatives ensured that the French Revolution came to play a major role in British politics. Edmund Burke's determined insistence that what happened in France was of direct relevance to Britain appeared somewhat implausible when he published his *Reflection on the Revolution in France, and on the Proceedings in Certain Societies in London Relative to That Event* on 1 November 1790, for France was then very weak. Burke's views soon, however, seemed vindicated by events because, as the Revolution became more radical, it nevertheless continued to attract a measure of domestic British support, culminating in December 1792 in an insurrection that was feared but that never occurred. The radicals who appealed to the French National Convention for support, sending, for example, petitions and other messages, played into Burke's hands, but, at the same time, their activities reflected a perception that they shared with Burke, namely that events in France were of direct relevance to Britain and that Britain was necessarily involved in a wider European struggle between the supporters and opponents of revolution. Indeed, Catholics during the Reformation, and Communists and Fascists during the Nazi-Soviet Pact of 1939–41, are but instances of a wider process in which opponents of the state aligned with hostile foreign powers, and very deliberately so.

Burke's analysis of direct relevance had been resisted by the Pitt ministry in the spring, summer and early autumn of 1792 when it had insisted on neutrality despite the outbreak of the French Revolutionary War. However, the entry of Britain into the conflict the following year transformed the situation. The Revolutionary and Napoleonic Wars reshaped British patriotism, strengthening its association with conservatism in place of its earlier eighteenth-century identification with reforming traditions. In 1797, the Reverend Edward Nares (1762–1841), Fellow of Merton College (1788–97) and Regius Professor of Modern History at Oxford (1813–41), preached a sermon on a day of public thanksgiving for a series of British naval victories. Published in 1798, it was dedicated to Elizabeth, Viscountess Bateman, the wife of one of his patrons, the combination of links reflecting the nature of what has been recently termed the English 'church-state'. Just as Burke had stressed the 'moral lessons' to be drawn from history, which he saw as involving the will of God, so Nares proclaimed history to be of value because it displayed the Providential plan, and, in terms that reflected the assessment of the current situation in Europe, he contrasted the historical perspective with the destructive secular philosophy of present-mindedness with its sense of the end of history:

> the enemy begin their operations on the pretended principle of giving perfect freedom to the mind of man. I call it a pretended principle, not only because their subsequent actions have been entirely in contradiction to it, but because, in fact no principle, as the world at

present stands, could be found more inimical to the real interests of human nature. For it is plain, that the first step to be taken in vindication of such a principle, is to discard all ancient opinions as prejudices; every form of government, however matured by age, is to be submitted afresh to the judgment and choice of the passing generation, and the Almighty to be worshipped (if at all) not according to the light vouchsafed to our fore-fathers, but as every short-lived inhabitant of the earth shall, in his wisdom, think proper and sufficient ... when the calamities of war befall us, we are not irrational in considering these also as under the direction of God ... The great point is to discover the heavenly purposes.

Nares's sermon, which paralleled the idiom of Anglican sermons in the Seven Years War, came to the reassuring conclusion that British victories proved divine support. The perception of Britain's imperial destiny as having both a Providential purpose and Providential endorsement was a central plank in the Church of England's public theology. Moreover, the French Revolution gave new energy to the defence of established Christianity. In 1805, Nares delivered the Bampton Lectures at Oxford, defending Christianity against 'modern infidels', and in 1808 and 1809 he was a select preacher at the university. Furthermore, in the face of the new challenge from Revolutionary France, there was much charity and sympathy for French refugees, including clerics. The Jesuit school for English Catholics, originally founded abroad at Saint-Omer in 1593, moved to Stonyhurst in Lancashire in 1794. Once atheistic France had been identified with the Antichrist, Catholics could appear as allies.

The defence of what was presented as the British system took a number of forms. The dedication to George III of the *Supplement* to the third edition of the *Encyclopaedia Britannica*, which was published in 1801, declared that it was designed to counteract the *Encyclopédie*, then seen as a precipitant of revolution.

The Revolutionary and Napoleonic period witnessed both a renewal of the ideological themes of the British *ancien régime* and the birth of modern British conservatism with its scepticism about the possibilities of secular improvement and its stress on historical continuity and national values, rather than present-mindedness and internationalism, or the alternative modern impetus behind British conservatism, the furtherance of capitalism and the concomitant defence of certain sectional interests. This Burkean conservatism was not necessarily restricted to Britain: Burke himself treated pre-Revolutionary Europe as a community and a commonwealth, was very concerned about the situation in France, and was averse to any peace with her that did not entail a counter-revolution. However, a stress on continuity, and therefore the value of specific constitutional and political inheritances, did not readily lend itself to serving as the basis of an international ideology.

Despite Burke's polemic about a European community being assaulted by the French Revolution and, earlier, by the powers that partitioned Poland, the appeal to history against reason was inherently nationalist. Indeed, one of the major intellectual problems facing the forces of conservatism or, as they later became, the 'right' in Europe during the Revolutionary–Napoleonic period and subsequently was the difficulty in formulating and sustaining an international ideology. The variegated nature of the *ancien régime*, its latent ideology of specific privileges, did not lend itself to this task, no more than did the xenophobic, provincial, proto-nationalist and nationalist responses to French power in 1792–1815. The continued failure of British conservatism to establish Continental links was to culminate in Britain's effective isolation within the European Economic Community in the late twentieth century, and in early 2016 in the extent to which Germany under Chancellor Merkel of the Christian Democratic Party (Germany's version of the Conservatives) found it relatively easy to brush aside pressure for change from David Cameron.

As with much of Europe, 'patriotism' in Britain in this period and thereafter was heavily and increasingly associated with anti-French and thus, from the early 1790s, to a considerable extent conservative sentiments. Correspondingly, in Britain, although not only there, conservatism was increasingly nationalistic in tone and content. The experience of the Napoleonic Wars in particular underscored a patriotic discourse on British distinctiveness while simultaneously creating a new iconography of national military heroes. Thus Robert Southey (1774–1843), who became Poet Laureate in 1813, developed the language of patriotism. War with France was justified on moral grounds. Southey also wrote patriotic accounts of Nelson, Wellington and the Duke of Marlborough. In the 1800s, 'God Save the King', which had first been sung publicly during the Jacobite crisis in 1745, came to be called the national anthem.

Britain played a major role in the rallying to Church and Crown that proved such a distinct feature of the 1790s and 1800s across much of Europe, and played a potent role in the definition of nationhood. The notion that objective national interests exist developed rapidly. In large part, it was a product of the eighteenth-century Enlightenment proposition that humans live in a universe governed by natural laws which proclaim, among other things, the existence of 'nations', defined through a mixture of geography, language, culture, physical features, even traits of personality; and that the 'interests of nations' essentially are to be defined in terms of protecting their geographical, cultural and physical (that is, relating to security) integrity.

Nationalism was not only a matter of long-term trends. The short-term crisis of the French Revolutionary period was also crucial. In Britain, Auckland called for a programme of indoctrination in order to achieve an acceptable politicisation of the country:

... every possible form of Proclamations to the People, orders for Fast Days, Speeches from the Throne, Discourses from the Pulpit,

85

Discussions in Parliament etc. I am sure that we should gain ground by this. The prosperity and opulence of England are such, that except the lowest and most destitute class, and men of undone fortunes and desperate pursuits, there are none who would not suffer essentially in their fortunes, occupations, comfort, in the glory, strength and well-being of their country, but above all in that sense of security which forms the sole happiness of life, by this new species of French disease which is spreading its contagion among us ... the abandoning of religion is a certain step towards anarchy.

This mixture of national identity, economic interest, religious conviction and a 'sense of security' was to prove very potent. Loyalism was a genuine mass movement, especially in England, even if it proved difficult to sustain the level of engagement, and the relationship between government and loyalism could be ambiguous.

However, there were many not comprehended within loyalism. Furthermore, there was in place from the 1770s onwards an alternative model of political order which posed a substantial threat to the ideological smugness of both Whig and, later, Tory elements in British politics. This alternative model was deployed with great effectiveness in the 1790s by the radicals, particularly Tom Paine, in a way that potentially undercut the attempt to tar radicalism with the slur of advocating pro-French principles. Thus the attempt to associate radicalism with Revolutionary France was, to a degree, a carefully orchestrated polemical move, rather than a wholly obvious and uncontentious one. Again, this served to underline the need for nuance in dealing with the clear-cut identification of certain assumptions and values as characterising the apparently uniform abstraction known as British opinion.

Imperial Britain

This was the age of Britain as *the* world power. Imperialism, moreover, has to be seen not only as the spread of British power but also in terms of its consequences, such as trade, migration and public attitudes. For political reasons linked to empire, divergence between Britain and the Continent was to be a major theme of the period covered in this chapter and notably up till the 1870s. It was a period when Britain concentrated on empire, while her colonial and maritime rivals suffered from defeat and colonial rebellion in 1791–1835, and from absorption in domestic strife and Continental power politics thereafter. Britain recovered rapidly from the loss of the Thirteen Colonies, West and East Florida, Minorca, Senegal and Tobago in the War of American Independence (1775–83) and the Treaty of Versailles (1783) to establish the first British foothold in Malaysia (Penang, 1786), and the first European colony in Australia (1788), and to thwart Spanish attempts to prevent her from trading and establishing settlements on the western coast of modern Canada (Nootka Sound Crisis, 1790). In contrast, the French took a long time to recover from the loss during the Revolutionary and Napoleonic period (1789–1815) of maritime power and colonial possessions and pretensions, while Spain and Portugal did not recover from the loss of their Latin American empires in the early nineteenth century. The Pacific became an area of increasing British interest, while India served as the basis of British power and influence around the Indian Ocean. The rise in British imperial power had a great influence on the British economy, on the British élite, who were provided with a new sense of role and mission and, in many cases, with careers, and on British public culture.

The sense of Britain necessarily playing a major role in resisting challenges to the European system, a sense that had characterised opposition to Louis XIV, the Revolution and Napoleon, ebbed. This was because empire increasingly set the themes of Britain's role and identity, a process that was greatly furthered by the development of widespread emigration to certain colonies. The establishment of the British imperial position owed much to contingent circumstances, principally relative success in war, and it was not surprising that the pantheon of imperial heroes defined and depicted in the nineteenth century was largely composed of military figures, such as Horatio Nelson, while the Duke of Wellington was the only former general in British history to become Prime Minister. Colonial expansion was generally welcomed, although the theme of the corruption, financial, political and moral, brought by such power was one that was sounded, not least by eighteenth-century critics of British activity in India, and by some opponents of the firm policies of George III towards his American colonies.

The nature of the British empire and of the European world altered dramatically in 1775–1835. In 1775 all English speakers were subjects of the British Crown, while the majority of such subjects outside Britain were white, Christian, of British or at least of European origin, and ruled with an element of local self-government, albeit not to the satisfaction of many in the Thirteen Colonies. Furthermore, predominantly Catholic populations posed problems, notably, but not only, in Minorca and Québec.

The American Revolution brought a permanent schism to the English-speaking world, though it ensured that aspects of British culture, society and ideology, albeit in greatly refracted forms, were to enjoy great influence, outside and after the span of the British empire. The modern role of the English language owes more to America than to modern Britain. The settlements and conquests of the period 1783–1815 also changed the character of the empire, not least by bringing numerous non-white and non-Christian people under British control. Some of these gains, such as Ceylon (Sri Lanka), the Seychelles, Mauritius, Trinidad, Tobago, St Lucia, and the 'land-islands' of Cape Colony, Essequibo and Demerara (British Guiana), were achieved at the expense of other European powers. Others, such as much of southern India annexed as a result of the Second and Third Mysore Wars (1790–2, 1799), or the protectorate over Oudh established in 1801, were gains at the expense of non-European rulers.

Naval power permitted Britain to dominate the European trans-oceanic world during the French Revolutionary and Napoleonic Wars. Danish, Dutch, French and Spanish naval power was crippled as a result of British victories, principally Copenhagen (1801 and 1807) over the Danes, Camperdown (1797) over the Dutch, and St Vincent (1797), the Nile (1798), and Trafalgar (1805) over the French and Spaniards. Britain was left free to execute amphibious attacks against the now-isolated centres of other European empires. British naval power helped to make French control of Louisiana redundant. Indeed, Napoleon's sale of Louisiana to the United States in 1803 was an apt symbol of the Eurocentricism that was such a characteristic feature of French policy after the failure of the Egyptian expedition as a result of Nelson's victory at the battle of the Nile (1798), although Napoleon also hoped that the sale would harm Anglo-American relations.

British success owed much to her naval power, but more to her insular status. Of the islands lying off the European mainland, only Britain was both independent and a major power. This allowed, indeed required, her to concentrate on her naval forces, unlike her Continental counterparts which, even if also maritime powers, as most obviously with France and Spain, devoted major resources to their armies. This concentration was crucial to Britain's success in defeating the Bourbons in the struggle for oceanic mastery in 1739–63: War of Jenkins' Ear with Spain, 1739–48; War of Austrian Succession with France (hostilities, 1743–8); Seven Years War with France, 1756–63 (hostilities begun 1754), and war with Spain 1762–3. It was also crucial to Britain's ability, first, to survive the attempt to reverse the verdict during the War of American Independence and, secondly, to resist Revolutionary France and Napoleon. As, however, in the case of conflict with Germany in 1940–45, political will, insular status and sea (and in 1940 air) defences were sufficient to maintain national independence, and would probably have led to the defeat of invasion attempts, but they were insufficient to defeat the rival state. For that, it was necessary to have powerful allies. London audiences applauded the final lines of George Colman's *The Surrender of Calais* when it was first performed in July 1791:

> Rear, rear our English banner high
> In token proud of victory!
> Where'er our god of battle strides
> Loud sound the trump of fame!
> Where'er the English warrior rides,
> May laurelled conquest grace his name.

That April, however, the government of Pitt the Younger had pulled back from the Ochakov Crisis, a confrontation with Catherine the Great over Russian gains from the Turks: the ministry and the political nation had been divided over the advantages and risks of such a war. It proved impossible in 1791 to sustain Britain's alliance with Prussia and the British policy of preventing territorial aggrandisement that might threaten the balance of power. Moreover, despite Britain's naval power, the Revolutionary and Napoleonic Wars with France were an extremely difficult as well as lengthy struggle, and it was by no means clear that French domination of Western Europe would be short-lived. The defeat of Napoleon in 1812–14 owed much to Austria, Prussia and Russia. It would have been impossible for Britain to have overthrown his Continental empire.

The British also, however, played an important role in Napoleon's eventual defeat, and about thirty thousand men annually joined the army. This was not in some way separate from British history in the nineteenth century but, instead, a formative experience for the British nation of that period. The decision to name a major London railway terminus (Waterloo, opened 1846) after Wellington's greatest victory was indicative of the lasting impact of the war. It complemented London's memorial to Nelson in Trafalgar Square. These sites, and the related occasions, contributed directly to a sense of national exceptionalism. The length of the struggle powerfully stamped it on the consciousness of experience, and the Conservatives were to derive a longer electoral and political benefit from the Napoleonic Wars than from the Second World War. Unlike Churchill, Liverpool continued to hold office long after the end of the conflict, until his stroke in 1827.

Initially, the British were badly affected by the military dynamism of Revolutionary France. British forces were less successful in the Low Countries in 1793–5 than they had been there in 1689–97, 1702–12, and even 1744–8, and in Germany in 1758–62. The French were in reasonably secure control of the Low Countries from 1795 until 1814, the longest period in British history when they were controlled by a hostile power. British challenges, in Holland in 1799 and in the Scheldt estuary in 1809, were both short-lived and unsuccessful, humiliatingly so, and even in 1814 things went wrong. In 1801–2, the British had to accept in peace negotiations French control of the region, which they had been unwilling to tolerate before the war in 1792–3.

Yet, aside from being politically stable compared to other European countries, Britain was the most successful of the European powers on the world scale. Multiple military capability was not restricted either to the Europeans or to the British, but Britain was the most successful of the European powers in developing and utilising such a capability. In part, this reflected British skill and success in naval, amphibious and trans-oceanic operations, and, in part, the cultural, political and geographical factors that led them not to place as great a premium as their European opponents on warfare on the Continent. Britain's role in the defeat of Napoleon climaxed at Waterloo in 1815. Napoleon surrendered less than a month after Waterloo to an astonished Captain Frederick Maitland of HMS *Bellerophon*. The British naval blockade made it impossible for him to leave France by sea. The British were concerned to prevent Napoleon taking refuge in America. He was taken, instead, to the British island of St Helena in the South Atlantic, where he died, his imprisonment a consequence and sign of British power.

Napoleon was not only defeated in Europe; France had also lost the struggle for oceanic mastery and colonial predominance. Thanks to repeated naval victories from the Glorious First of June in 1794 on, the British had been left free to execute amphibious attacks on the isolated colonial centres of non-European powers, and also to make gains at the expense of non-European peoples. The route to India was secured: Cape Town was captured from the Dutch in 1795 and, after it had been restored in 1802, again in 1806. The Seychelles were taken in 1794, Réunion and Mauritius in 1810. The British were able to consolidate their position in India. Seringapatam, the capital of the Sultanate of Mysore, which had been a serious foe since the 1760s, was stormed in 1799. The booty included a pair of bronze cannon which flank the stairway at Powis Castle. India became the basis of British power and influence around the Indian Ocean, and it proved possible to expand the colony that had been founded at Botany Bay in Australia in 1788. The Pacific became a sphere for British, rather than Spanish, expansion.

The Congress of Vienna, which sought in 1814–15 to settle the problems of the European world, left Britain with a dramatically stronger position. Her control of Cape Colony, the Seychelles, Mauritius, Trinidad, Tobago, St Lucia, Malta, Surinam and Ceylon (Sri Lanka) was all recognised, and France's position within Europe was weakened. The European territorial settlement, notably in the Low Countries, reflected British interests. Britannia ruled far more than just the waves.

London also was the capital of a growing empire. Turning away from Europe's conflicts gave Britain the opportunity to expand elsewhere. Equilibrium in Europe provided opportunity, and a sense of opportunity further afield. Wellington was Prime Minister in 1828–30, while Trafalgar Square, begun in the 1820s, soared with Nelson's column, which was topped by Edward Baily's eighteen-foot-high statue. The bronze lions followed in 1867. Nelson monuments were also erected in Dublin and Edinburgh, while his victorious death at Trafalgar was commemorated in paintings, portraits, engravings, medallions and dinners.

The distinctive feature of the post-medieval European empires was their desire and ability to project their power across the globe: by the late eighteenth and early nineteenth centuries, Britain was clearly the most successful in doing so. There was an interesting parallel with Russia. Both powers were in a way outside Europe, able to a considerable extent to protect their home base or centres of power from other European states, yet also able to play a major role in European politics. Their geopolitical isolation should not be exaggerated. With reason, British governments feared invasion on a number of occasions from 1690 to 1813, and again thereafter from the mid-nineteenth century on. Russia was invaded, by Sweden in 1708–9 and by Napoleon in 1812, attacked, as by Sweden in 1741 and 1788, or threatened, as by Prussia and Britain in 1791. Nevertheless, their strategic position was different from that of other European states: just as they had avoided the ravages of the Thirty Years War, so they were to see off Napoleon and thus thwart the last attempt before the age of nationalism to model anew the European political space.

In almost every other respect—social, economic, religious, political—the differences between Britain and Russia were vast. The histories of the two countries before and since the early nine-

teenth century have been utterly dissimilar. Thus, their geopolitical similarity at this juncture, in marked contrast to the rest of
Europe, is a caution against assuming that in all criteria Britain
was closest to nearby parts of Europe and against too great a stress
on the consistent parallel developments of different states, as
opposed to more short-term convergences and divergences.

By 1815, most of the trans-oceanic European world outside
the New World and, as a result of the rebellions in South and
Central America, by 1830, the vast majority of all European possessions abroad were British, and some of the others, most obviously the Dutch East Indies and, later in the century, the
Portuguese in southern Africa, were in part dependent and protected territories. The situation was not to last; indeed, 1830 was
the date of the French occupation of Algiers, the basis of their
subsequent North African empire. Nevertheless, the unique
imperial oceanic position that Britain occupied in the Revolutionary, Napoleonic and post-Napoleonic period was to be of
crucial importance to the economic and cultural development of
the state in the nineteenth century.

The nineteenth century was Britain's century, not only because
of her imperial and economic power, but also because, although
Britain experienced fundamental socio-economic changes, which
brought considerable dislocation and hardship, she did so without revolution or sustained social disorder. Although the failure
to integrate Ireland successfully into Britain and its future were
serious problems, the nineteenth century was the first in which
'the British problem' did not lead to war or insurrection. The
economic advantages of Union were too apparent for many Scots
to doubt its advantage. Britishness was presented as offering a
civic understanding of nationhood, not an ethnic one. The
British empire, indeed, proposed a union of values, and not of
place or race.

Many of the special assets which Britain enjoyed or developed
were subsequently to dwindle, disappear or become liabilities.

Her insular position and imperial role; early, comparatively labour-intensive industrialisation; the dominance of London; and rule by Crown-in-Parliament, have all proved mixed blessings. To some contemporaries, Britain's success appeared challenged, threatened, even precarious; and it may now appear to have been both precarious[1] and short-lived. But, while it lasted, it was real, even if flawed. Nineteenth-century Britain had much in common with her neighbours, but, for a while, she followed a path as distinctive as sixteenth-century Spain or the United Provinces (Netherlands) in the seventeenth century.

1851 saw a great celebration of Britain's success. The Great Exhibition was an impressive tribute to the majestic products of manufacturing skill and prowess. Planned by Prince Albert in 1849, it was seen by him as a demonstration of British achievement and as reflecting 'England's mission, duty, and interest, to put herself at the head of the diffusion of civilisation and the attainment of liberty'. The Exhibition revealed in an acceptable format some of the results both of the Industrial Revolution and of the territorial revolution created by the rise of the British empire.

At the time of the Great Exhibition, James Wyld built a large model of the globe. 'Wyld's Great Globe' was exhibited in a large circular building in Leicester Square in 1851–62. Gas-lit, it was sixty feet high, about forty feet in diameter, and the largest hitherto constructed. No eccentric, Wyld was an active parliamentarian, Master of the Clothworkers' Company, and a leading promoter of technical education. He reflected a widespread British confidence in Britain's superiority and rule. In the *Notes to Accompany* his globe, dedicated to Prince Albert, Wyld wrote: 'What comparisons suggest themselves between the condition of the Pacific region in the time of Cook and now? What was then held by illiterate savages now constitutes the rising communities of New South Wales ... the civilizing sway of the English crown ... an empire more extended than is governed by any other sceptre.'

Empire was not simply a matter of power politics, but also military interests, élite careers and an ideology of mission that appealed to the propertied and proselytising. The Protestant churches of Britain devoted their resources to missionary activity outside Europe, particularly, though not only, within the empire, and not to proselytism on the Continent, while Continental Protestant churches had only small-scale missionary activity, principally Lutherans in India and South-East Asia. A sense of mission, often linked to or expressed in racial and cultural arrogance, was a characteristic also of the imperialism of other European states, as well as of the Americans in the USA and subsequently in the Pacific, and of expatriate Europeans, such as the Australians in their interior and in the south-west Pacific.

Most clearly in the final decades of the century, empire had relevance and meaning throughout British society, as was reflected in the jingoistic strains of popular culture: adventure stories, the ballads of the music hall, and the images depicted on advertisements for mass-produced goods. Empire reflected and sustained the widespread racist assertions and assumptions of the period, both of which were amply demonstrated in its literature. Newspapers spent substantial sums on the telegraphy that brought news of imperial conflict. Launching the Boy Scout movement in 1908, Robert Baden-Powell exploited his own reputation as a war hero in the Boer War (1899–1902), celebrated by the press, and the model of masculinity allegedly provided by the self-sufficiency and vigour of life on the frontiers of empire. The sieges of the Indian Mutiny (1857–9) and the Boer War offered drama for the entire country, although that did not imply that imperialism was popular with all the working class. Many workers appear to have been pretty apathetic. The crowds that applauded the relief of Mafeking in 1900 from Boer siege were mainly clerks and medical students, rather than labourers.

If empire was a crucial component of British nationalism, especially towards the end of the century, it was also of great economic importance, both for exports and for imports. The difficulty of competing in Europe and the United States, and of expanding sales in traditional colonial markets in Canada and the West Indies, ensured that the bulk of the rise in exports in 1816–42 was obtained from markets in Africa, Asia and Latin America, areas of formal and informal empire.

As a result of the end of protection for British agriculture with the repeal of the Corn Laws in 1846, and of the technological changes, including steamships, refrigerated ship holds (in the 1880s), barbed wire and long-distance railways, that led to the development of agricultural production for the European market in other temperate climates and to the ability to move products rapidly without spoilage, Britain in the 1870s and 1880s became part of a global agrarian system. Britain had been agriculturally self-sufficient in 1815, but from the 1860s cheap grain imports greatly affected British agriculture. For food imports, Britain looked to empire, both formal and informal—New Zealand, Canada and the Argentine—rather than to the Continent of Europe. Grain from Germany, Poland and the Ukraine, the latter two both ruled by Russia, was only purchased in significant quantities in some years. Some Continental agricultural products were important in Britain, most obviously fruit and vegetables, German sugar-beet, and Danish bacon and dairy products, and by the end of the century Danish bacon and eggs were the staple of the British breakfast. Nevertheless, it was North American grain, Argentine beef and Australasian wool and mutton that were crucial. In addition, Britain became a vital market for these producers. About half of all Canadian exports by value in 1891–1915 were wheat and flour for Britain, and timber was also important.

More generally, English became the lingua franca of business, the language of profit, across most of the world, a development that owed much to expatriate communities and to the role of British finance and shipping and, later, although to a lesser extent, air transport. By 1835, the *British Packet and Argentine News* was an established weekly in Buenos Aires, with a strong mercantile emphasis. It regularly reported the movement of foreign ships and the current prices of such commodities as skins, wool and salt. The major rival as a lingua franca was French, which in many respects was more important on the Continent until at least 1917.

A major difference between Britain and Continental countries, especially in the mid-nineteenth century, was that Britain traded abroad far more than they did, and far more widely. Her leading industrial sectors, textiles and metal products, were dependent on exports. Continental economies were more self-sufficient; what foreign trade they did was mainly with other European countries, including Britain. As a result of this contrast, Britain was dependent on foreign trade, and on the wider world outside Europe, in a way they were not. This was related to other aspects of Britain's distinctiveness: her outward-lookingness and internationalism; her interest in peace, which was believed to create the best conditions for trade; and her opposition to a large and expensive army. For Britain, free trade was an ideology and a policy, a goal and a means.

From 1815, there was, for Britain, no struggle for survival to focus loyalism and discredit radicalism. The reconceptualisation of national and imperial greatness, so that it did not focus so closely on fortitude and triumph in war, as it had done in 1793–1815, provided opportunities for Whig and Liberal presentations of Britishness in terms of reform. Whereas the wars had fostered a sense of national exceptionalism, the emphasis after 1815 was on success in a process of change that was scarcely limited to Britain.

Empire and free trade were later to coexist with difficulty but, in the third quarter of the nineteenth century, they were both part of the official ideology of the strongest political and economic power in the world. Vulnerable foreign powers were persuaded or forced into accepting free trade agreements: Turkey in 1838, Egypt and Persia in 1841, and China in 1842. Thailand (1857), Japan (1860) and Morocco followed. The successful imperialism of free trade reflected the triumph of a free-trade tariff system and the dynamics of imperial expansion, although during the heyday of free trade the formal empire (over which political control was exercised) played a relatively small role in the British export-import economy. Those who pushed free trade hardest, for example Richard Cobden and John Bright, were most hostile to the formal empire as it was, and were opposed to its expansion.

The role of free trade as a popular creed, and as a commitment to low indirect taxation on the necessities of life, was peculiar to Britain. As the USA was later to show in the 1940s, free trade held particular attractions for the leading trading and financial power. Sterling, on the gold standard from the 1820s, was the major currency used in international trade and finance. It was the reserve currency and medium of exchange. From the 1820s, Britain exported vast quantities of investment capital, and this played a crucial role in the rise of the City of London as the leading world financial centre. Britain's position as the leading exporter of manufactured goods to non-European primary producers, aided by the interest from her foreign investments, funded economic growth and investment.

In Britain, however, free trade furthered a major transfer of power away from agricultural interests and regions. A similar shift of power and influence from land to industrial, commercial and, particularly, urban wealth and ideas occurred on the Continent, although, as in Britain, this process was resisted in aristocratic, landed and military spheres. The attempt by the Conservative-dominated British House of Lords in 1909 to thwart the 'People's' Budget, with its 'super-tax' on the wealthy and its taxation measures on landownership, was eventually over-come by the Liberals. There were similar political and social tensions on the Continent.

Empire and crucial global economic links scarcely suggest that Britain had much to do with the Continent. The dynastic link with Hanover was broken in 1837, and Prince Albert's early death in 1861 cut short his influence. Thereafter, the reign of Victoria was the longest period since that of Elizabeth without a foreign-born royal consort. Albert was a friend of the Prussian royal family and took a closer interest in European power politics than Victoria. Nevertheless, Victoria still took a very close inter-est in Continental power politics, in which she had a family role. She turned for advice to her uncle, King Leopold I of Belgium, and felt close to his wife, Louise. They often met in the late 1830s and 1840s. Victoria married her relatives into the Continental royal families and became the matriarch of the European monarchies: Kaiser Wilhelm II of Germany was her grandson. Nevertheless, despite popular jibes about the 'German' royal family, they were thoroughly English by 1900—the claim that Edward VII, George V and Queen Mary spoke with German accents has been disproved.

Britain was, in relative terms, militarily stronger than she had ever been before. Her naval forces were under considerable pres-sure because of rising commitments and concern about the actions and plans of other powers, but, from Trafalgar (1805) onwards, Britain was supreme at sea. Demonstrations of naval strength, such as the Spithead Review of 1853, greatly impressed contemporaries. Thanks to this strength, Britain was able, to a considerable extent, to feel insulated from Continental develop-ments and to be free to intervene elsewhere in the world. India indeed was the basis for a British land empire, so that Britain was a 'dual monarchy'.

Continental Links

Yet it would be misleading both to overlook nineteenth-century Britain's links with the Continent and to treat her in isolation. If Britain's global responsibilities meant that she took a view of the world in which Europe was simply one element, it was nevertheless a very important one. The concept of the 'balance of power' from the eighteenth century and that of the 'Concert of Europe' in the nineteenth indicate how central the Continent was in the conduct of British foreign policy. In particular, British ministers played a crucial role in the peace settlement of 1815 agreed at the Congress of Vienna.

As earlier, after the Peace of Utrecht (1713), ministers were thereafter concerned about the fate of the settlement and about other international developments. Thus, the unravelling in 1830 of the attempt in 1815 to create a strong and stable state in the Low Countries, in the form of a greater Netherlands, led to British diplomatic action designed in particular to deter an increase in French influence. There was also concern about Portugal, a traditional ally, and in 1827 British troops were sent to Lisbon when the government was threatened by a Spanish-supported insurrection. George Canning, Foreign Secretary from 1822 to 1827 and, briefly, Prime Minister in 1827, and, later, Henry, 3rd Viscount Palmerston followed Continental developments closely, and crises in Spain and Greece led to particular interest. British ministers were very worried about what they saw as French aggression—in Spain in the 1820s and 1830s, in the Near East in 1840–1, in Italy and on the Rhine in the 1850s and 1860s. Canning protested without success in 1823 when French troops helped suppress a liberal revolution in Spain.

In the case of Canning, support for national interests ensured that a general non-interventionism was tempered by a considerably more active stance in particular contexts. Thus, the attempt to distinguish isolationism from interventionism is problematic. So also for individuals. For example, in 1872, Benjamin Disraeli pressed for caution about expensive expansionist projects, only to be more bellicose by the late 1870s.[2]

Imperial issues could have a European dimension, most obviously with 'the Eastern Question', created by Turkish weakness and Russian ambitions in the Balkans and the Near East. British opposition to Russian expansion led to the Crimean War (1854–6) and later to threats of conflict in the 1870s and 1880s. The terms 'jingoes' and 'jingoism' were coined in 1878 as a result of a music-hall song by 'the Great MacDermott', the chorus of which started, 'We don't want to fight, but by jingo if we do, we've got the ships, we've got the men, we've got the money too', a refrain that continued to be sung into the twentieth century. Yet, concern over Russia focused on the broader question of Indian security, rather than on Russian dominance of Eastern Europe.

Britain was no more insulated economically than politically. Economic growth did not mean that there were no fears of Continental economic competition. British commentators were aware of the benefits and drawbacks of reliance on Continental grain. There was a dangerous Continental grain mountain until the 1830s, and then an even more worrying general shortage, and this change was one of the major reasons for the repeal of the Corn Laws in 1846. Concern about German commercial competition was also a significant factor. In the parliamentary debates of February–March 1839 on the Corn Laws, in response to the depression, almost every speaker was aware of the threat from foreign manufacturing, especially because of the Prussian-led German Zollverein (Customs Union). The Zollverein's tariffs against British manufactured imports led to frequent protests from British manufacturers and merchants.

The Continent was not only a source of competition. Free trade was always the real British interest because she traded so much not only with her empire, but also with the whole world, including the Continent, which, for much of the nineteenth century, was Britain's best market. In the mid-century, British notions of economic liberalism were influential in much of Europe, although anxiety about British dominance of international trade encouraged protectionism.

For Britain, reliance on empire alone for trade was never feasible, as most commentators were aware. Instead, Britain exported to the Continent large quantities of finished goods, particularly machinery, woollens and metal products, as well as semi-finished manufactures, such as yarn. Prohibitions on the export of machinery were repealed in 1843, and machinery exports were accompanied by technical information and advice, managers and large numbers of British workers to operate the machines. In the third quarter of the century, British exports to the most rapidly industrialising parts of Europe rose further than overall export growth, although this was reversed during the following quarter. In the Edwardian period, Britain's second most important export market (after India) was Germany.

Technological change, meanwhile, had brought the outer world much closer, enabling the more rapid and predictable movement of messages, people and goods. In 1821, the Dover–Calais packet service was converted to steam. Thirty years later, the first messages were sent through the new submarine cable between Dover and Calais.

Cultural Links

Links were not only of the type of exports of British locomotives. More generally, educated Victorians were acutely aware of what they shared with other European peoples as a result of a common culture based upon Christianity and the legacy of ancient Greece and Rome. Gladstone published three books on

Homer. Edward, 14th Earl of Derby, Prime Minister in 1852, 1858–9 and 1866–8, was a Classical scholar of note. He delivered part of his inaugural speech as Chancellor of Oxford in 1853 in Latin and translated Homer's *Iliad*. Sir John Herschel, a leading scientist, translated the *Iliad*, as well as Dante and Schiller. The British élite idealised their perception of ancient Greece, and the growing number of public schools made the Classics the centre of their teaching. The British élite saw itself as modern counterparts of the Athenians and Romans.

The Classics were not alone. Those who could afford to do so performed and listened to German music, read French novels, and visited the art galleries of Italy. Continental works were also available and influential in translation. Thus, the Scottish writer James Thomson published important translations of Heine and Leopardi, both of whom influenced his work. His poem 'The City of Dreadful Night' (1874), the leading work of Victorian pessimism, took its motto from Leopardi. Similarly, Victorian melodrama drew heavily on Continental sources. The plot of *London by Night* (1843), a work attributed to Charles Selby, was based on Eugène Sue's *Les Mystères de Paris* (1842–3); while *The Corsican Brothers*, the success of 1852, was based on Alexandre Dumas the Elder's novel *Les Frères corses* (1845).

Melodrama, however, also testified to the resonance of hostile images of foreigners. Thus, in William Travers's *The Dark Side of the Great Metropolis* (1868) a wicked French madame inveigled unsuspecting British virgins into her brothel. The villainous Rigaud in Charles Dickens's novel *Little Dorrit* (1855–7) was a 'cosmopolitan gentleman' of Swiss and French parentage, born in Belgium, 'a citizen of the world'.

Travel abroad was not just exhilarating: it was also regarded as a crucial aspect of a civilised upbringing. George III had never gone abroad, but Victoria visited Louis-Philippe in 1843, and in 1845 accompanied Albert revisiting the scenes of his youth at

Coburg, Gotha and Bonn, and meeting the rulers of Belgium and France. In her later years, Victoria travelled to the Continent, particularly France, almost every year; she even held a 'summit meeting' with the leading German minister, Bismarck, in 1888. Her son Edward VII was a frequent traveller, particularly happy in France.

At a very different social level, mass foreign tourism grew apace, in part thanks to the pioneering development of the tourist industry by Thomas Cook. For all, foreign travel helped to create or strengthen images of other places and countries. Venice inspired Byron (who gave his life to the cause of Greek independence), Browning and Ruskin. Wordsworth was greatly influenced by the *idea* of Italy, a fusion of Classical civilisation and landscape and hopes of modern regeneration, and engaged with Italian poets, moralists and historians; while Dickens, a keen supporter of Italian independence, devoted much space in the journals he edited to Continental topics. In contrast, Spain only became familiar to British artists and the British public after the painter David Roberts's travels in the 1830s. In the mid-century, the notion of Spain as colourful and exotic was popularised by the artists John Phillip and John Burgess. Meanwhile, a growing number of tourists arrived in Britain, although their numbers never approached those of Britons going abroad.

Britain was open to Continental influences in many fields, not least music. Haydn had been a great success on his visits in 1791–2 and 1794–5, and Spohr was invited over in 1819 by the Philharmonic Society, which also commissioned Beethoven's Ninth Symphony. Rossini had mixed success, but made much money in 1824, and Weber composed his opera *Oberon* for Covent Garden in 1826, only to die of tuberculosis in London soon after the successful opening. Johann Strauss the Elder and his orchestra came over for Victoria's coronation in 1838 and were extremely successful, and in 1847 Verdi produced his new opera *I Masnadieri* at Covent Garden with great success. Continental pianists, such as Franz Liszt in 1827, Henri Herz and Sigismond Thalberg, were very popular in London. In 1840–1, Liszt returned and toured Britain, playing in Dublin, Edinburgh and the English provinces, as part of an ad hoc cosmopolitan tour that included a British musical comedian and a French prima donna. Mendelssohn and, later, Dvořák were especially popular in Britain. Mendelssohn's *Elijah* was written for the 1846 Birmingham Festival. Offenbach's operettas reached London in the 1860s, Johann Strauss the Younger's *Die Fledermaus* in 1875.

Edward Dannreuther introduced the concertos of Chopin, Grieg, Liszt and Tchaikovsky to London audiences and organised Wagner programmes. Charles Hallé, a German conductor who had studied and worked in Paris, came to Britain as a result of the 1848 revolution and in 1858 founded what was to become a famous orchestra in Manchester. The Hallé's fame rose under the conductorship of Hans Richter, a Hungarian conductor who had trained in Vienna and been a conductor at Munich, Budapest and Vienna, as well as giving a series of annual concerts in London from 1879 until 1897.

While we should not regard interest in foreign music uncritically as a sign of cosmopolitanism, it is important to note that the British celebrated their own nationality in this praise of the foreign music. Composers who were willing to pander to British taste, such as Mendelssohn in his oratorios, were cultivated. Verdi was popular in large part because he was seen as a liberal nationalist defying autocracy and the Papacy. Indeed, his operas could be seen to offer a model of why Britain was superior. Similarly, Pedro V of Portugal pleased Queen Victoria when he visited her at Osborne House because, although he went to Mass, he criticised the ignorance and immorality of Portuguese society and praised Britain.

British composers were also influenced by their Continental counterparts. Mendelssohn's oratorios spawned a host of imitations. Composers thought of as quintessentially English were open to foreign influences. Hubert Parry, the son of a Gloucestershire landowner who collected Italian Primitives, was trained by Dannreuther and greatly influenced by Brahms and Wagner, writing an *Elegy for Brahms* and attending the 1876 Bayreuth *Ring* cycle in company with Bruckner, Saint-Saëns and Tchaikovsky. Arthur Sullivan studied music at Leipzig. Edward Elgar was greatly influenced by Brahms and Wagner, Frederick Delius by the writings on art of the German philosopher Nietzsche. Brahms and Wagner were most influential from *c.*1880 until 1914. Wagner's development of the vocabulary of music to the ultimate point of tonality and his exploration of chromaticism were of importance for British music, while his belief in the need for reconciling art and the community was very influential among intellectuals from *c.*1880 until 1914. His exploration of mythology and psychology in his musical dramas anticipated Freud and Jung and influenced D.H. Lawrence, T.S. Eliot and James Joyce. George Bernard Shaw used Wagner's *Ring* in order to support his critique of capitalism.

British culture had less influence on the Continent. Dickens for example was read more in America. British art and music did not set the tone abroad. Nevertheless, there were influences. Shakespeare was important for French Romanticism and very influential in the development of Russian realism, and Chekhov, Dostoevsky and Turgenev were greatly influenced by him and more generally by British culture. Chekhov was impressed by British liberalism and technology, while Turgenev visited London frequently, was impressed by Byron, Scott and Dickens, stayed with Tennyson, knew George Eliot and received an honorary DCL at Oxford. British interest in Russian culture, for example the popularity of Chekhov, Dostoevsky and Turgenev, did not extend, however, to support for the policies of the Russian state, which were often condemned as cruel and aggressive, as in Swinburne's 'Ballad of Bulgarie'. Indeed, the contrast between cultural links and political criticism is more generally the case. Care is necessary before reading from these links to approval of the society in question.

Political Concern

The British people were involved in what was happening politically on the Continent. This was obviously true of the Napoleonic and Crimean Wars, but, in addition, the Greek War of Independence and the Risorgimento (Italian unification) aroused enormous interest—more so than many of the minor British colonial wars and acquisitions of colonial territory. The Tory *Morning Post* referred critically in 1829 to 'the spurious sentimentality so prevalent both in England and France on the subject of Greece'. The local newspaper in William Bell Scott's painting *The Nineteenth Century, Iron and Coal*, finished in 1861, carries an advertisement for a 'Grand Panorama!!! Garibaldi in Italy. Struggles for Freedom ...', a show that ran in Newcastle that March. The painting also included a poster advertising 'prime Rotterdam hay'. Great attention to foreign affairs was displayed in the press throughout the century.

The manner in which the Italian hero Garibaldi was applauded by working-class crowds when he visited England in 1864 testified to the way in which Victorians of all social classes were able to relate many of the events taking place on the Continent to their own struggles and aspirations. Garibaldi could not land at Portsmouth because the crowds were too great. Biscuits were named after him. This ability to relate was especially pronounced in the case of radicals, many of whom had strong internationalist views. London workers in 1850 were angered by the visit of

Julius Haynau, an Austrian general who had played an allegedly cruel role in the suppression of the 1848–9 Hungarian revolution. He was mobbed by a crowd of London draymen. The failure to relieve General Gordon at Khartoum in the Sudan in 1885, a colonial cause célèbre, caused outrage, and this imperial failure was a major blow to the popularity of Gladstone's second government, but in 1876 Gladstone had been able to embarrass Disraeli's ministry seriously over the massacre of Bulgarians by the Turks. The atrocities had a considerable impact on diplomatic, religious and intellectual relations with the Continent.

Yet interest in Continental affairs was also patchy. This was especially true of Eastern Europe. Violent events, such as the Polish risings against Russian rule in 1830 and 1863 or the Bulgarian massacres, could arouse concern, but it was generally occasional, and little was known about much of the Balkans or the Ukraine.

Nevertheless, although more attention was devoted to imperial questions from the 1870s, Continental news remained very important in the British press. George Alfred Henty (1832–1902), a war correspondent and popular author of adventure stories for boys, covered the Austro-Italian and Franco-Prussian wars, the Paris Commune and the Carlist revolt in Spain, although he also followed such heroes of empire as Napier and Wolseley on their African campaigns. Several of Henty's earlier stories dealt with themes from European history, but, in the preface of his *With Wolfe in Canada: The Winning of a Continent* (1887), he stressed Britain's trans-oceanic destiny, adding: 'Never was the shortsightedness of human beings shown more distinctly than when France wasted her strength and treasure in a sterile contest on the continent of Europe, and permitted, with scarce an effort, her North American colonies to be torn from her.' Henty's stories, such as *Under Drake's Flag* (1883), *With Clive in India: or, The Beginnings of an Empire* (1884), *St George for*

England: A Tale of Cressy [Crécy] and Poitiers (1885), *Held Fast for England: A Tale of the Siege of Gibraltar* (1892), *Under Wellington's Command* (1899) and *With Kitchener in the Soudan* (1903), continued to enjoy substantial sales until after the Second World War and to be frequently borrowed from public libraries in the 1960s. They contained some upright foreigners, for example French partisans during the Franco-Prussian War (1870–1), but the British were best.

This was generally the case in popular fiction. In Anthony Hope's novel *The Prisoner of Zenda*, the British publishing sensation of 1894, which was set in the fictional kingdom of Ruritania in Germanic Middle Europe, the British hero, Rudolf Rassendyll, was an exemplary foil to the villains, Black Michael and Rupert of Hentzau, a role he repeated in the sequel, *Rupert of Hentzau* (1898).

Nationalism and Xenophobia

Interest in the Continent, frequently strong, was not incompatible with a sense, generally very pronounced, of British superiority. The perfectibility or perfection of the British constitution was asserted. As reform legislation was passed within Britain, so British imperial power spread (not that there was a causal relationship), to the approval of British commentators. The two processes were fused as, first, internal self-government and, later, dominion status were granted to some British colonies. New Zealand achieved self-government in 1852, Newfoundland, New South Wales, Victoria, Tasmania and South Australia in 1855, Queensland in 1859, and the dominion of Canada in 1867.

It is scarcely surprising that an optimistic conception of British history was the dominant account in academic and popular circles. This was helped by the generally pacific character of the Chartist reform movement in the late 1830s and 1840s, and the failure of its attempt to use extra-parliamentary agitation to put pressure on Parliament. Linked to this, the 'Year of Revolutions'—1848—was, in Britain, peaceful compared to the widespread, violent disturbances and numerous changes of government on the Continent. A progressive move towards liberty was discerned in Britain past and present, a seamless web that stretched back to Magna Carta in 1215 and other episodes which could be presented as the constitutional struggles of the baronage in medieval England, and forward to the extensions of the franchise in 1832, 1867 and 1884. These were seen as arising naturally from the country's development. Writers such as Macaulay played a major role in renewing the Whig interpretation of history. He had a phenomenal world readership and helped to focus attention on the 'Glorious Revolution' of 1688 as a crucial episode in the development of Britain. Macaulay's influence contributed to earning him a peerage.

This public myth, the Whig interpretation of history, offered a comforting and glorious account that seemed appropriate for a state which ruled much of the globe, which was exporting its constitutional arrangements to other parts of the world, and which could watch convulsions on the Continent as evidence of the political backwardness of its states and of the superiority of Britain. The leading British role in the abolition of the slave trade and the emancipation of the slaves also led to self-righteousness, while Evangelicalism further encouraged a sense of national distinctiveness and mission. The peaceful experience of Dissent in nineteenth-century Britain was also distinctive. Protestant Dissenters had a major impact on the whole fabric of society: disestablished religion contributed significantly to the 'progressive' ethos of eighteenth- and nineteenth-century Britain.

Religious toleration was seen as a major aspect of the Whig inheritance. Indeed, the Whig government of Viscount Melbourne (1835–41) in part depended on the support of Irish

Catholic MPs: in the 1830s there were at least 40 Catholic MPs, all bar one sitting for Irish constituencies. Although a devout Anglican, Victoria was ready to attend Presbyterian services in Scotland, where she was head of that established church, and Lutheran services in Germany, and she saw herself equally as the monarch of all her subjects, whether Hindu, Jewish or of any other faith. Her Proclamation to the People of India of 1858 repudiated any right or desire to impose on the faith of her subjects and promised all, irrespective of religion, the rights of law. In 1868, Victoria visited a Catholic Mass in Switzerland and in 1887 Pope Leo XIII was allowed to send an envoy to congratulate Victoria on her Golden Jubilee: the Queen was conspicuously gracious to him. On her state visits to Ireland in 1861 and 1900, Victoria met the heads of the Catholic hierarchy, and Lord Salisbury's second government had in the Home Secretary, Henry Matthews, the first Catholic cabinet minister since the seventeenth century.

The peaceful situation in England, Scotland and Wales, but not Ireland, contrasted with the bitter divisions in French, German, Italian, Spanish and Portuguese society and their recent histories of internal conflict and revolution, which made it far harder to imagine a convincing account of long-term and unitary national development.

Victorian Britain displayed a sense of national uniqueness, nationalistic self-confidence and a xenophobic contempt for foreigners, especially Catholics. This xenophobia can, however, be seen in terms not of a hostility to foreignness per se, but rather as one to what was seen as backward and illiberal. These characteristics were defined in accordance with British criteria, but these criteria were also seen as possessing wider applicability. Thus, hostility was based on a system of values, not on racialism. It was the lack of 'liberty' on the Continent that was most criticised. Thus, as with the earlier use of Protestantism to define values and nationhood, the criteria applied to judge Continental societies in the Victorian period could also be used to criticise aspects of British society.

Conversely, foreigners and foreign ideas could be acceptable. The rejection of foreigners and foreignness was deep-rooted, but it did not prevent Disraeli, whose paternal grandfather was an Italian Jewish immigrant, from becoming Prime Minister. Somewhat differently, Sir John Seeley, Regius Professor of Modern History at Cambridge, both emphasised the role of imperial expansion in modern British history in his *Expansion of England* (1883) and reflected his interest in German culture and history in his *The Life and Times of Stein* (1878).

As so often, however, national confidence was tempered by concern. Confidence was most developed in the 1850s and 1860s, which were abnormally prosperous decades, and even then it was not unqualified. Concern arose from a number of causes, each of which was of varying effect: strategic, political, economic, cultural and religious. It is easiest to place an explanation and a date on the first two because they left clear markers in governmental, parliamentary and newspaper records. A more active France was a source of anxiety, and invasion by her, thanks to a 'steam[ship] bridge' from Cherbourg to Portsmouth or through a planned Channel tunnel, was feared in 1847–8, 1851–2 and 1859–60.

Yet, it was in alliance with France, as well as with Sardinia-Piedmont and Turkey, that Britain fought Russia in the Crimean War (1854–6). This was the last war that she waged with a European power until the First World War broke out in 1914, a length of time unprecedented since the Norman Conquest. Britain lacked the large European army necessary to compete effectively in European power politics and, as in the early modern period, the eighteenth century, 1793–1815, 1914–18 and 1939–45, required a powerful ally to help were she to seek to do so. While the British navy displayed its strength in its wide-ranging attacks on Russia during the Crimean War, the army's weakness was demonstrated and its prestige lessened, not least when Sebastopol fell to the French in 1855 rather than the British. Britain had earlier co-operated with France and Russia in supporting Greek independence under the Treaty of London of 1827. Such co-operation, however, proved short-lived. The Anglo-French alliance broke down before the Crimean War ended, and British suspicion of Napoleon III was markedly revived.

The emphasis by Disraeli, Prime Minister in 1868 and 1874–80, on the Conservatives as a national party offered a defining contrast with what was presented as the cosmopolitan rootlessness of other political groups, the Whigs and Liberals, and those Conservatives who, according to Disraeli, were led astray. Notable among the last group was Sir Robert Peel, Prime Minister in 1834–5 and 1841–6, who repealed the protectionist Corn Laws in 1846. Disraeli's organic concept of Britain as a community, the originator of one-nation Conservatism, was not limited in time. Indeed, history was deployed to criticise radicalism as well as interventionism. Pitt the Younger's support for peace, imperial preference and low taxes was also useful to Disraeli. An interest in better relations with France, which Disraeli pursued in 1852, made sense in this context.[3] He wanted co-operation with France in order to resist Russian expansion, and criticised Palmerston, the Whig foreign policy panjandrum, for alienating France. Seeking economy, Disraeli, nevertheless, was no isolationist. He argued that it was necessary to preserve the appropriate system and situation on the Continent as well as in Britain.[4]

There was a consistent strand, both during the nineteenth century and more generally, of opposition to over-mighty powers and defending the existing system. However, the policy prescriptions adopted were different, as more generally with engagement with the Continental states. There could be a stress on intervention or, more modestly, action or, alternatively, on caution. The same range was also true for relations with the United States. The need for the containment of international disruption had been outlined in 1858 in a circular from James, 3rd Earl of Malmesbury, the talented Foreign Secretary, who argued that, as peace 'cannot be disturbed in any quarter without the risk of the disturbance becoming more general', Britain would therefore 'always be ready, by her good offices, to contribute to moderating angry discussion, to avert hostile collisions, or to remove entanglements which may threaten to alienate nations from one another'.[5]

Contrasting views were the case in British public debate more widely. For example, alongside a belief in toleration, a sense of religious challenge reflected concern about the position of Catholics in Britain, and church–state struggles on the Continent were followed closely. Anti-Catholicism was given fresh impetus by the growing strength of the Catholic Church in Ireland and, in particular, by developments in Britain: Irish immigration, the Oxford Movement, the re-establishment of a Catholic hierarchy, and the revival of papal dignities in 1850. Pius IX's bull restoring the Roman Catholic hierarchy in England was issued without consultation with the government, and the situation was exacerbated by the triumphalist note struck by the new Archbishop of Westminster, Cardinal Wiseman. Prominent 'old Catholics', such as the Duke of Norfolk, disapproved of his new zeal for public activity.

Anti-Catholic sermons, publications, petitions and rallies were matched by renewed vigour in the celebration of the Fifth of November, Guy Fawkes Night. The Ecclesiastical Titles Act, passed in the Commons by 433 votes to 95, banned the new hierarchy in 1851. Public tension over religious questions increased appreciably. A Catholic street procession was attacked in Stockport in 1852, and in 1867 the army was called in to deal with disturbances following anti-Catholic public meetings in Birmingham.

The Oxford Movement, a High Church movement launched in 1833 that affirmed Catholic liturgy and doctrine within the limits of Anglicanism and opposed secular power, led to the Church of England becoming fearful of a fifth column. This was strengthened when two of the leaders, John Newman in 1845 and Henry Manning in 1851, converted to Roman Catholicism. Thereafter, those who remained within the Church of England and sought to transform it from within—Anglo-Catholics and Puseyites—were even more urgently seen as possible traitors.

Victoria was unhappy with the views and ceremonial innovations of the Puseyites and hostile to appointing them bishops. The situation in the early 1850s led to a shift in the Queen's position towards Catholics. In her early years, she had been conciliatory and, in 1850, Victoria declared that she could not bear to hear violent abuse of Catholics. She told her children not to share in the 'vulgar prejudice' against Catholics. In 1848 the British government had offered Pius IX asylum on Malta when he was faced by serious disturbances in Rome. Victoria's position then hardened and by the early 1870s her private attitude was somewhat like that of a Protestant crusader; she strongly disapproved of conversions to Catholicism, for example those of the 3rd Marquis of Bute in 1868 and of the Marquis of Ripon in 1874. In her final years, there was a second dramatic transformation and Victoria became in some respects a philo-Catholic.

As a reminder that relations with the Continent were not solely a matter of British attitudes and policies, anti-Catholicism was also heightened by developments abroad. Pope Pius IX (1846–78) stated the doctrine of the Immaculate Conception (1854), issued the bull *Syllabus Errorum* (1864), which criticised liberalism, and convoked the First Vatican Council (1869–70), which issued the declaration of Papal Infallibility. All these moves appeared to vindicate traditional views of the reactionary nature of Catholicism and served, in Britain and elsewhere, to increase suspicion about the intentions of the Catholic Church and the loyalties of Catholics. In Germany, this led to the *Kulturkampf* (culture struggle) of 1873–87 as the government attacked the position of the Catholic Church: the Falk Laws of 1873 subjected the church to state regulation.

There was nothing comparable in Britain, but it was clear that Catholic Emancipation—the repeal of civil disabilities to which Catholics were subject—in 1829 had not ended religious tension. Indeed, in 1837, the Duke of Newcastle introduced into the Lords a bill to repeal Catholic Emancipation. It was defeated, but it testified to concern about religious questions and a continuing sense among many Protestants that national identity was synonymous with British Protestantism.

Views on the Catholic challenge and on divisions among Protestants found greater depth by contesting the past, notably the causes, course and consequences of the Reformation. The providential account of the overthrow of Catholicism faced criticism not only from Catholics, but also from within Protestantism, and not only by the Anglo-Catholics. The dissolution of the monasteries came in for particular criticism due to its impact on social welfare.[6] These disputes underlined the centrality of religious concerns to British relations with the Continent. The situation appears different today, although the historians of the future may well find that religious views played a role in attitudes towards European links, albeit for fewer people than in the past.

There was also a degree of intellectual rivalry between Britain and the Continent. Berlioz might have adored Shakespeare, but influential nineteenth-century Romantic and nationalist Continental philosophers, such as Hegel and Nietzsche, looked down on the pedestrian and unphilosophical English. Byron, who did make a positive impact, had left Britain in disgrace. Nevertheless, Walter Scott was a renowned figure on the Continent. Furthermore, British liberal thinkers were influential. This was especially true of Scottish Enlightenment thinkers, particularly Adam Smith, but also Ferguson, Robertson and Miller, while Jeremy Bentham had a major European reputation. His works were published in French, German, Portuguese and Spanish, and he was involved in Greek politics in the 1820s. Mill's liberalism was widely influential. Britain was an attractive model to nineteenth-century Germans, not least because her constitution and development could be interpreted in different ways and her example thus appropriated by different political tendencies.

The British in turn were affected by Continental intellectual developments. German literature, philosophy, theology, and Classical and philological studies were followed with great attention. Coleridge introduced both Kantian ideas and German critical theory to Britain. He visited Germany in 1798 and 1828, and on the former occasion attended lectures at Göttingen. Greatly influenced by Kant, Schiller, Schelling and both August Wilhelm and Karl Wilhelm Friedrich Schlegel, Coleridge was an important exponent of the principles of German Romanticism. Other writers were also greatly influenced by German Romanticism. The Scottish historian, philosopher and critic Thomas Carlyle produced a *Life of Schiller* (1823–4) and a translation of Goethe's *Wilhelm Meister's Apprenticeship* (1824). He later offered a heroic view of the famous king of Prussia in his most ambitious work, *The History of Frederick the Great* (1858–65). Ranke, and German historical scholarship in general, had a major impact on British historians. Hegel was influential from the 1880s. Nietzsche's thesis that art could enable man to live in a world without God, his justification of the artist, and his idea of the 'superman' were influential from about 1900 and affected D.H. Lawrence for instance.

Liberal German biblical scholarship was more influential than Nietzsche, reflecting the significance of religion in this period. This scholarship affected British intellectuals from the 1850s and, in particular, the 1870s on as biblical (textual) criticism came into English scholarship. Higher Criticism, the study of the Bible as literature, challenged the literal interpretation of Scripture. David Friedrich Strauss (1808–74) contradicted the historicity of supernatural elements in the Gospels in his *Das Leben Jesu* (1835–6). This was translated by the English novelist George Eliot as *The Life of Jesus, Critically Examined by Dr David Strauss* (1846) and led to the loss of her faith. She also translated *Das Wesen des Christentums* (1841) of Ludwig Feuerbach, as the *Essence of Christianity* (1854). Feuerbach saw religion as the product of self-alienation and the projection of ideal qualities onto an invented 'other'.

German biblical scholarship affected Anglican christology as well as the Anglican doctrine of the atonement and view of human nature. It also led English Presbyterianism and Congregationalism to move away from orthodox Calvinism. By 1910, their theology was more liberal and less Calvinistic than it had been in the 1860s. These changes were controversial and resisted by traditional thinkers, but, by 1914, even Anglo-Catholics were equivocating on such earlier staples as the Fall, original sin and the doctrine of the atonement. Protestantism was loosened up as the traditional authority of the Bible was challenged, while the right of private judgement in religious matters was increasingly stressed by Protestants. These shifts also reflected the inroads on conventional religious beliefs made by scientific developments and, in particular, Charles Darwin's theory of evolution, as well as the impact of a more optimistic view of human nature.

Nationalism played a major role in a sense of distance from the Continent, not simply because of British attitudes, but also because of the development of a consciousness of national identity, politically, economically, culturally and ethnically, in the Continental states of the period. The reign of Victoria was the age of the unification of Germany (1866–71) and Italy (1860–

70). Furthermore, under the Third Republic established in 1870 many of the debilitating domestic divisions that had challenged French political stability since the 1780s were eased or expressed peacefully. Political reform on the Continent ensured that by 1865 some European states had more extensive franchises than Britain. Despite the absence in England of a paramilitary police force, there was probably little difference in policing strategies between London and Paris, while any notion of a specifically more benevolent model has to take note of Ireland. Whether they had a 'democratic' facet or not, Continental states increasingly seemed better able to challenge British interests.

Irish nationalism was a major problem for the British state, one that posed serious issues of civil order in Ireland and of political management at Westminster. As a result, Britain faced questions that bore some relation to those of other 'multiple states' affected by internal nationalist pressures, most obviously Austria-Hungary and Russia. Moreover, it thereby contrasted with states that did not face similar problems of diversity and where nationalism could more easily serve to reflect and unite the country, for example France. This underlines the extent to which contrasts are not always between Britain and the Continent but among European countries, with Britain simply on one side.

The Challenge of European Rivals, 1870–1914

The process of late Victorian imperial expansion and economic growth took place in a context of European competition that was far more serious and gave rise to far more concern than the position in 1815–70, worrying as that had been at times. The international context was less comforting than in the third quarter of the nineteenth century. This was due to the greater economic strength of the major Continental powers, their determination to make colonial gains in pursuit of their own place in the sun, and the relative decline in British power. These factors combined and interacted to produce a strong sense of disquiet in British governmental circles, as well as an increase in popular hostility to foreign countries and peoples.

At the close of the nineteenth century there was less confidence in Britain (let alone the Continent) that British institutions and practices were best, and a sense in Britain that reform was necessary. The 3rd Marquess of Salisbury, Conservative Prime Minister in 1885–6, 1886–92 and 1895–1902, was not alone in being pessimistic about the future of the empire.

The tremendous growth in German power, and an accompanying increase in her international ambitions towards the end of the century, posed a challenge to Britain, in whose governing circles there had been widespread support for German unification and a failure to appreciate its possible consequences. The philosopher and historian David Hume, travelling through Germany in 1748, had written to his brother, 'Germany is undoubtedly a very fine Country, full of industrious, honest People, and were it united it would be the greatest Power that ever was in the World.' There had, however, then seemed little prospect of this, not least because of Austro-Prussian rivalry.

By the 1870s, the situation was very different and Germany came to seem a model for change. More established political rivals, France and Russia, were also developing as major economic powers, while American strength was ever more apparent in the New World and, increasingly, the Pacific. The leading imperial challenges to Britain of c.1870 to c.1902 were French and Russian. The Continent was from c.1885 to c.1903 locked in an effective balance of power or diplomatic stalemate: Germany and Austro-Hungary versus France and Russia. Hence there was the impetus and opportunity to turn to extra-European expansion.

The major powers competed in part by expanding their influence and power in non-European parts of the globe, a sphere where rivalries could be pursued with a measure of safety and without too substantial a deployment of resources. As a result, and given the importance of imperial considerations in British governmental, political and popular thinking, it is not surprising that British relations with, and concern about, the Continental powers registered not so much in disputes arising from European issues, as in differences and clashes centring on distant, but no longer obscure, points on the globe, ranging from Fashoda in the forests of the Upper Nile to the islands of the western Pacific. By 1900 the British had an empire covering a fifth of the world's land surface and including 400 million people.

Between 1815 and 1851, while other European states made only modest colonial gains, the British empire expanded across several continents. India was the most important area of expansion. The British also expanded in Malaya, gaining Malacca and Singapore, and annexed Aden in 1839, the first time it had been captured by a European power. British warships moved into the Persian Gulf, while Argentinian and American interest in the Falkland Islands was countered by their occupation by the British in 1832–3. Success against China in the Opium War led to the acquisition of Hong Kong in 1842. The British presence in Australia and New Zealand spread. In South Africa, the British expanded from Cape Colony, and Natal was annexed in 1845.

Territorial expansion provided raw materials, markets and employment, and, combined with evangelism, encouraged a sense of Britain as at the cutting edge of civilisation. The country's destiny increasingly seemed imperial and oceanic. The varied consequences included the ability to send plant-hunters all over the world, enriching British gardens with plants never seen before in Britain, and encouraging the creation of arboreta to display trees from far-flung places. British capital and expertise played a major role in many parts of the world. Banking houses such as Barings provided the credit for the development of railways abroad, as with America's first railroad, the *Baltimore and Ohio*. The British also exported to the world. Coal from ports such as Cardiff, Seaham, Hartlepool and Sunderland powered locomotives and forges elsewhere. Activity was a key theme. It linked Britain to the wider world, but without providing a sense of similarity.

Both political and ideological expression were part of the process, and took many forms. The creation of the title of Empress of India for Victoria in 1876, a response to the transformation of the Prussian kingdom into a German empire, was followed by wars with the Zulus and Afghans and by confrontation with Russia. The last was seen by Disraeli as a necessary response to Russian expansionism even if it exposed Disraeli to criticism for being the enemy of Christian interests. In practice, Disraeli was in line with a foreign policy tradition emphasising a pragmatic defence of interests in which empire and Europe both took a part, but with each interpreted with reference to particular conjunctures. The defence of British prestige, national interests and empire were Disraeli's ideas, and he saw them as closely linked. Moreover, his imperial solidarity with the Turks, as well as contempt for the Balkan Christian rebels, was typical of a conservative British approach to Balkan events.[7]

Much British imperial expansion in 1880–1914 arose directly from the response to the real or apparent plans of other powers, although the search for markets was also important. Thus both economic and political security were at stake, and the 'imperialist phase' has been seen as marking the beginning of the long decline from the zenith of British power. Sovereignty and territorial control became crucial goals, rather than influence and island and port possessions, which had been the characteristic features of much, although by no means all, British expansion earlier in the century. Suspicion of Russian designs on the Turkish empire and French schemes in North Africa led the British to move into

Cyprus and Egypt; concern about French ambitions led to the conquest of Mandalay (1885) and the annexation of Upper Burma (1886); while Russia's apparently inexorable advance across Central Asia led to attempts to strengthen and move forward the 'north-west frontier' of British India and the development of British influence in southern Persia (Iran) and the Persian Gulf. French and German expansion in Africa led Britain to take counter-measures, in the Gambia, Sierra Leone, the Gold Coast, Nigeria and Uganda.

Specific clashes of colonial influence interacted with a more general sense of imperial insecurity. In 1884, there was concern about British naval weakness and the increase in the French navy. In 1889, public pressure and the need to give credibility to Mediterranean policies obliged the government to pass the Naval Defence Act, which sought a two-power standard—superiority over the next two largest naval powers combined. Expenditure of £21.5 million over five years was authorised. The importance of naval dominance was taken for granted. It was a prerequisite of an ideal of national self-sufficiency that peaked in the late nineteenth century.

By the turn of the century, it was Germany, with its great economic strength and its search for 'a place in the sun', that was increasingly seen as the principal threat. Carlyle had received the Order of Merit of Prussia as a result of writing to *The Times* on behalf of Prussia in the Franco-Prussian War; but, in 1871, the collapse of the French Second Empire the previous year inspired *The Commune in London*, a pamphlet that foresaw a successful Prussian invasion of Britain and the establishment of a republican commune in London. Many British commentators were then more concerned about France and, in particular, Russia, but the situation was to change. In 1897, Wilhelm II and his government gave a new thrust to German colonial expansion in their *Weltpolitik*. In December 1899, the rising journalist J.L. Garvin decided that Germany, and not, as he had previously thought, France and Russia, was the greatest threat to Britain. Rejecting the view of Joseph Chamberlain, Secretary of State for the Colonies, that Britain and Germany were natural allies, their peoples of a similar racial 'character', Garvin saw 'the Anglo-Saxons' as the obstacle to Germany's naval and commercial policy.

British resources and political will were tested in a major naval race between the two powers, in which the British launched HMS *Dreadnought*, the first of a new class of battleships, in 1906. A projected German invasion was central to *The Riddle of the Sands* (1903), a novel by Erskine Childers, which was first planned in 1897, a year in which the Germans indeed discussed such a project. The Anglo-French entente of 1904 was followed by military talks with France aimed at dealing with a German threat. Their consequences were to play a major role in leading Britain towards the First World War. As another reminder of multiple links, Frederick, 16th Earl of Derby, who in 1904 had become President of the British Empire League, agreed in 1907 to preside over the Franco-British Exhibition in London.

Russian defeat in the Russo-Japanese war of 1904–5 weakened Russia as a balancing element within Europe, thereby exposing France to German diplomatic pressure, and creating British alarm about German intentions, as in the First Moroccan Crisis of 1905–6. This crisis, provoked by Germany, was followed by Anglo-French staff talks aimed at dealing with a German threat. Their consequences were to play a major role in leading Britain towards the First World War. In 1907 British military manoeuvres were conducted for the first time on the basis that Germany, not France, was the enemy. That year fears of Germany contributed to an Anglo-Russian entente.

Yet, as was customary, political opinion was divided. Alongside hostility to Germany in political and official circles, there were influential politicians, such as the 5th Marquess of Lansdowne, Foreign Secretary in 1900–5, his fellow Liberal-Unionist, the Earl of Selborne, First Lord of the Admiralty, and Lord Sanderson, Under-Secretary at the Foreign Office, who sought to maintain good relations, although Lansdowne also negotiated the entente with France. Wilhelm II was given an honorary degree by Oxford. The ententes indeed were not alliances. In one light, Britain failed to make her position clear, thus encouraging Germany to hope that she would not act.

Britain and the Continent towards the Close of the Period

The states that were vying for position at the turn of the century were also changing rapidly. Britain in the late nineteenth and early twentieth centuries experienced social changes similar to those of the Continent. Although the Church of England still played a major role in society and had not suffered heavily from involvement in contentious politics, as the Church had done in France (where it was disestablished in 1905), Germany and Italy, its political, religious, intellectual and educational authority had been challenged. Britain shared in a more general disestablishment and secularisation.

Similarly, as on the Continent, a hierarchical society and its values coexisted with rapid social change. Throughout Europe, there were significant transformations, both cause and consequence of societies with spreading education and political rights, and widespread urbanisation and industrialisation. These brought social dislocation, instability and anxiety, expressed in part in Britain, as on the Continent, by hostility to immigrants. Deference and traditional social patterns ebbed. Privilege coexisted with meritocratic notions, and greatly expanded institutions that, within limits, reflected such notions—the civil service, the professions, the public schools, the universities and the armed forces—played a role in the creation of a new social and cultural establishment different from the traditional aristocracy.

Working-class political consciousness and activism developed markedly in Britain, as on the Continent. It was also characterised by a sense of international solidarity that drew on a tradition in British radicalism from the 1790s on. As then, with the favourable and hostile responses to the French Revolution, there was a sense of parallels and links in domestic political developments throughout Europe, although there were relatively more working-class leaders who were 'international' in outlook in France and Germany. Nevertheless, the British Labour and Socialist movements, and, in particular, leaders such as Keir Hardie and Ramsay MacDonald, had genuine links with Continental counterparts. These were stronger than the links between 1918 and 1939 and even more so than post-1945 connections.

Yet, there were also major differences. British Liberalism could, and can, be seen as a mass movement similar to Continental republicanism or socialism, but it was hardly republican or socialist, and even as a mass movement it needs qualifications, given its leadership from within the governing élite. In addition, the British Labour–Socialist movement was very much on the periphery of the Second International: Marxism was decidedly weak in Britain compared with most Continental countries. By Continental standards, the Liberal Party was particularly popular and its Conservative rival notably liberal. This contrast was more generally true in British political history. Movements did not match those with which they might appear aligned, and attempts to make comparisons can overlook this point.

Notions of similar development challenged any sense of British uniqueness, although, as already mentioned, such a sense had been challenged before, most obviously by the awareness of common Protestantism from the sixteenth century, so that

England, or Scotland, was only one of the elect nations. Similarly, in Victorian and Edwardian Liberal or, even more, Socialist eyes, British disputes had an international dimension. If the conservative notion of an organic British or at least English system was to be contested, it was necessary to resort to universal principles, and reasonable to look abroad for examples. The direction of such a search was confined. Whereas, in the 1980s, it was to be considered appropriate to turn to Japan for examples of labour relations and industrial organisation, in the late nineteenth and early twentieth centuries the only other developed industrial states were in Europe and North America.

The British attitude towards America was ambivalent. Thanks to the steamship, the Atlantic shrank: crossings became faster, more comfortable, safer and more predictable. In 1914, it took only a week to cross between Britain and the United States, as compared to six weeks in the 1850s; and the sinking of the *Titanic* in 1912 led to casualties among an Anglo-American élite that shared much in terms of values and experiences. Of the as many as 24 million people who emigrated from the British Isles between 1815 and 1924, far more left for the United States than for Continental Europe.

Many Victorians wrote about this new land. Independence had been followed by a considerable measure of divergence as a separate national American culture was established, although there were significant regional differences. Dickens, Trollope and the historian James Bryce were all taken by America's energy and drive, yet often shocked by its populist politics, which were seen as vulgar and dangerous. A standard means of criticising a politician was to accuse him of the 'Americanisation' of British politics, and Gladstone and Chamberlain both suffered accordingly.

It is possible to stress both convergence and divergence between Britain and the Continent when discussing the period 1815–1914. Similar social and economic trends impacted upon different cultures. Industrialisation in the Donbass was not the same as industrialisation in Silesia or Lancashire. Yet the overall impression is one of converging experiences, not least in terms of demography. Similar transformations were planned and executed in the major European cities, including the construction of underground railways and major road systems. Public education and, later, low-rent housing programmes were designed to cope with the disruption of urbanisation and social change.

In addition, the functional similarity in domestic power relationships between Britain and the Continent in the eighteenth century was, in some respects, increasingly matched in the field of political thought and governmental ideology. It is necessary, however, to be cautious before assuming any general, smooth and gradual increase. Furthermore, it is similarly important to be cautious about assuming progressively greater British interest in Continental developments. Instead, for example, British interest in French domestic politics has been seen as becoming less apparent, so that the constitutional innovations of 1875 aroused little response. Nevertheless, even if political, legal and institutional traditions separated Britain from Continental states, they had problems, as well as responses, in common. Utilitarianism was not an attitude constrained by particular constitutional traditions. As a consequence, comparisons appeared more pertinent. Thus, Sir John Acton Bt, then a Liberal MP close to Gladstone, later the distinguished historian Lord Acton, wrote in an essay on nationality in the *Home and Foreign Review* of July 1862, 'If we take the establishment of liberty for the realisation of moral duties to be the end of civil society, we must conclude that those states are substantially the most perfect which, like the British and Austrian Empires, include various distinct nationalities without oppressing them.' Thus, in this case, alongside a stress on British excellence there was a readiness to search for a Continental comparison. As Acton was a Catholic with a German mother and a German-Italian wife, who had been educated at the University of Munich, he was especially open to Continental influences.

Acton, however, was not alone in looking abroad. Edwin Chadwick looked to French practice when urging changes in the policing of Britain. The Royal Commission, established in 1839, on which he served proposed a national police force, responsive to local authorities but managed nationally. Chadwick, who was the architect of the Poor Law Amendment Act of 1834 and was later appointed one of the commissioners of the new Board of Health set up under the Public Health Act of 1848, was criticised for his interest in professional administration from the centre and for drawing on foreign methods, a criticism also made of Prince Albert, but the willingness of 'progressive' thinkers to look abroad was instructive. Specifically, Prussian administrative practice held a strong appeal in the mid-century, as can be seen in the work of Carlyle; and even Dickens was attracted by Prussian centralism in the 1850s and 1860s. It is indeed possible to discern a common framework in administrative developments, for example in policing in England, France, Prussia and the USA, although distinct 'national traditions and experience' were also crucial. The 1839 and 1856 Constabulary Acts did not institute a national police or even a national system of management. There was much interest in the German educational system in the 1890s and early 1900s, and the national efficiency movement looked to German models.

A willingness to look abroad was not restricted to administrative principles and practices, but was true, more generally, of education. Military thinking was dominated not by Britain's experience of colonial warfare, but by discussion of Napoleon's campaigns in Italy and in 1813–14, and the wars of German unification in 1866 and 1870. In 1890 Spenser Wilkinson, then a leader writer for the *Manchester Guardian* and later the first Professor of the History of Warfare at Oxford, published *The*

Brain of an Army, which was a call for the formation of a General Staff on the German model.

The intellectual world of the eighteenth and early nineteenth centuries had not been closed to Continental influences, especially in Scotland; and even Oxford, so often derided in part on the basis of Edward Gibbon's acerbic remarks, had a justified European-wide reputation. Nevertheless, in the second half of the nineteenth century, Continental influences increased, in philosophy, political and economic theory, and science. Hegel's work had an impact on Oxford while, in the 1880s, Marx's views were disseminated in English. In 1883 H.M. Hyndman's *The Historical Basis of Socialism in England* appeared, offering a view of class development that drew heavily on Marx. In 1885, the group variously termed the 'Hampstead Marx Circle' or 'Hampstead Historic Society', which included George Bernard Shaw and Sidney Webb, began meeting to discuss Marx's work, which they approached through the French translation. Two years later, an English translation of *Das Kapital* appeared in London.

Britain shared in the artistic movements of the late nineteenth and early twentieth centuries. Just as the French Impressionists reacted against the particular conventions of academic painting, so their British counterparts, such as the 'Glasgow Boys', James Guthrie, E.A. Walton and W.Y. Macgregor, adopted a new and vigorous style, which in their case drew on the French Barbizon School and the French naturalist artist Bastien-Lepage. Thanks to the dealer Alexander Reid, who was painted by his friend Van Gogh, the Glasgow artists acquired international sales and reputation, while Degas and the Impressionists were introduced to Scotland.

At the same time, British writers played a role in the *fin de siècle* movement. The Irish writer Oscar Wilde wrote his play *Salome* in French in 1891. An English translation with illustrations by Aubrey Beardsley first appeared in 1894, but, as the play was banned by the Lord Chamberlain, it was first performed in Paris in 1896. In turn, *Salome* inspired Richard Strauss's opera, first performed in 1905. At a distance from the avant-garde, other arts were influenced by Continental developments and practitioners. Franz Winterhalter and Jacques Tissot were key figures in Victorian fashionable portraiture, although John Everett Millais, a British painter, was also important.

Continental work in science, especially in chemistry, a field in which the Germans made considerable advances, attracted British attention. Science held the key to the future, to the creation and use of goods, new sources of power, new sounds and substances. It ensured a world in which change was constant and possibilities apparently endless with the important exception of the continuation of the present. Technological change ensured the need for frequent retooling in order to retain competitive advantage. This had serious economic consequences, but also placed a serious burden on any state anxious to support its international position. Thus, warships became obsolescent far more rapidly than in the past. Technological change had a similar effect on other powers. More generally, the volatility of life encouraged both optimism and concern. Change did not separate Britain from the Continent, but then, alongside these links, the United States was also highly important to Britain, as was the empire.

Conclusions

The nature of relations between Britain and the Continent during the long nineteenth century is particularly important as they help set a context for subsequent views. Earlier relations are obscure for most people today, but the Victorian and Edwardian heyday of empire very much helped set assumptions, if not norms, for what followed. The extent to which these assumptions themselves were realistic, for then and later, is very much open to debate, but it would be foolish to underrate the significance of the earlier period for the twentieth century. It was important not only for its imperial aftermath, but also for the way in which relations with Europe in the long nineteenth century are not prominent retrospectively. That, again, created a misleading and problematic legacy, one reminiscent of a more general tendency to simplify the past.

In reality, Britain was very much linked to the Continent economically and culturally, at the same time that it was more politically and geopolitically separate than in any other recent century. Empire was both expression and cause, but also only an aspect, of a more varied situation.

5

THE TWENTIETH CENTURY

War, hot and cold, and then the European Union, dominate the standard perception of Britain's relations with the Continent during the twentieth century—understandably so. Although different, these were transformative experiences, and the last has become highly divisive. These issues indeed will be discussed, but they can drive out other important elements that are germane to Britain's relationship with the Continent and also provide valuable background and contexts for it. The range of these elements is immense. The relationship is at once political, ideological and cultural, including, for example, Britain's continued role as an imperial power into the 1960s, and the influence of ties with the United States; and also social in the form of the development of mass tourism to the Continent in the 1960s, and large-scale immigration from there in the 2000s and 2010s. Every community in Britain has been affected. Mass tourism to the Continent has provided experiences for most families. It led to the establishment of 'little Britains' in the Mediterranean, notably on the coast of Spain, but there was also a response to aspects of local society and certainly to local landscapes. Many British people also have purchased second homes on the Continent, notably in France and Spain. The Channel Tunnel, opened in 1994, was scarcely an equivalent to the land bridge severed in about 6500 BCE, but far more people have passed through it.

These factors interacted with those of identity. Many, but far from all, British people both felt themselves to be European and, in part as a consequence, were aware of differences as well as similarities. Moreover, social, economic, political, cultural and other trends, as was only to be expected, played out differently within Britain. The differences were social, political, geographical, and by age. On average, relations with the Continent were closer for the young than for the old, for the wealthy than for the poor, for graduates than for others, and for Londoners than for those in the North. The common trend, however, is that links became more contentious in the 2000s and, even more, 2010s, as relations with the European Union came to the fore in British politics and, in the late 2010s, to a degree that helped to define as well as reflect identity and political belief.

None of that appeared plausible, or even possible, at the start of the twentieth century. Trade then with the Continent was significant, there were important cultural links and, in 1904, there was a political alignment with France in the Entente Cordiale. Nevertheless, the prime form of identity was that of Britain as the great world empire. This identity very much drew on ideas of the British as living both in the British Isles and in the empire, notably the dominions.

The political aspects of this relationship were to be very prominent during the world wars, but had already been seen in the Boer War of 1899–1902, with contingents going from the dominions to serve in South Africa and being honoured on their return.[1] Indeed, the manpower of the empire appeared to answer one of the great conundrums of British exceptionalism in the early twentieth century, namely how Britain was to compete with other European great powers while avoiding conscription. The contrast reflected, and affected, social norms as well as political culture.

The World Wars

Empire was crucial for Britain and its survival and eventual victory in both world wars. At the same time, alliance with other European powers, notably France in the First World War (1914–18) and the Soviet Union in the Second World War (1939–45, but only from 1941), as well as with the United States, from 1917 and 1941, was also fundamental. Britain entered each world war to protect a European power to which it had made a public commitment in response to German aggression: Belgium in 1914 and Poland in 1939. This was not only the ostensible cause, but also a reflection of a long-standing drive, urgent in these circumstances, to prevent any one power from dominating the Continent. As such, Britain offered a definite model of European power politics. This model can be presented in cynical terms as serving to protect British interests, but far more was involved and was seen to be involved. Notions of balance and honour each played a role in 1914 and 1939.

The world wars saw large numbers of British men serving abroad, far more than ever before, and more dying there than ever before. Moreover, the conflict was followed accordingly on the 'home front', notably through correspondence and in the press, as well as in new media, especially newsreels. In the First World War, most troops on the Continent served in Belgium and France, but others fought in Italy and in northern Greece.

Britain played a major role both in achieving victory and in the negotiation of the peace settlement, notably the Peace of Versailles in 1919. Britain was also a major participant in the Russian Civil War (1918–21), playing a key role in helping secure independence for Estonia, Latvia, Lithuania and Finland, but failing to prevent the Soviet takeover of Ukraine and the Caucasus. This was a more far-flung intervention than in the Crimean War. It was not followed, however, by more lasting intervention. Indeed, foreign policy did not push European links to the fore in Britain's identity or interests in the two decades that followed the First World War.

Alongside empire, there was a strong sense of national identity, one in which the Continent did not play a role. In the 1930s, in opposition to the Communists and to Oswald Mosley's British Union of Fascists, which he presented as un-British, Stanley Baldwin, the Conservative leader until 1937, stressed national identity, continuity, distinctiveness and stolid common sense, and set a moral tone.[2] Baldwin did so not in order to embrace political reaction, but rather to seek an imaginative way to lessen tensions arising from economic change, particularly rivalry between capital and labour. Similarly, Labour kept a distance from the Communists.

The cultural context for a conservative depiction of national identity was strong in the 1930s, when films and newsreels offered an optimistic emphasis on social cohesion and patriotism, while most of the fiction that was read and the music that was listened to did not engage with Modernism. A patriotic history was offered by writers of the period, such as the historian Arthur Bryant, who, although atypical in his overt sympathies for Nazism,[3] was typical of many conservative inter-war British writers in seeking to represent and sustain an inherent patriotism. In doing so, Bryant and others, in a way that prefigured the present but in a very different context, confronted deep tensions within conservatism, notably in response to socio-economic changes and to mass culture. There were also the problems of defining a popular middle-brow voice and then using it to revive the nation. Historical writing and journalism were deployed to emphasise national roots in a way that was designed to be relevant not simply to the privileged few, but to all countrymen. This project had a sound basis in inter-war British society.[4] The Continent did not really play a role.

Far more than the First World War, the Second World War transformed the content, image and history of the engagement with foreign policy and the outside world. The previously dominant Conservative tradition was discredited as an aspect of the critique of Appeasement, although it would be mistaken to read the Conservative foreign policy of the previous half-century solely in terms of a non-interventionism construed as Appeasement. That would not, for example, adequately describe the diplomatic activism of Austen Chamberlain as Foreign Secretary from 1924 to 1929. This was an activism that looked back to an opposition to Russian expansionism seen in the 1710s, but one given greater ideological energy and direction in the 1920s by hostility to Communism and the conviction of its wide-ranging malign activism.

Although noted for saying that Czechoslovakia was distant and little known to the British, Neville Chamberlain, Prime Minister from 1937 to 1940, was capable of striking an internationalist note, as in his much-applauded speech on 3 October 1938 defending the Munich agreement. He referred to the importance of the agreement being carried out 'under the supervision of an international body'. Chamberlain's (eventual) internationalism can also be seen in his belief in a quasi-Concert of Europe and in his alienation from Germany after it breached the Munich agreement by occupying Czechoslovakia in March 1939.

Going to war over Poland led to a bold prospectus for action. Opposition to Germany was recast as a clearly idealistic struggle. On 3 September 1939, as the declaration of war was debated, Winston Churchill told the House of Commons:

> This is not a question of fighting for Danzig [Gdansk] or fighting for Poland. We are fighting to save the whole world from the pestilence of Nazi tyranny and in defence of all that is most sacred to

man. This is no war for domination or imperial aggrandisement or material gain, no war to shut any country out of its sunlight and means of progress. It is a war, viewed in its inherent quality, to establish on impregnable rocks, the rights of the individual, and it is a war to establish and revive the stature of man.

The war very much forced the public to engage with the reality of European power politics. British forces again played a key role in fighting in Western Europe and Italy, adding the Netherlands and Norway to the battlefields of the First World War, as well as more of France, Greece and Italy than in that struggle. The British also played an extensive role in naval and air conflict. The bombing of British and German cities brought a particularly bitter pressure to the 'home front', providing a parallelism of a certain type. At the same time, more British troops served outside Europe than in the previous conflict, notably in North Africa and in South-East Asia.

The Second World War also left politicians across the political spectrum with a far more interventionist tradition, notably with a degree of commitment to European power politics that did not accord with more accustomed imperial roles. In June 1940, the idea of an indissoluble union of Britain and France, with shared sovereignty, a single cabinet and Parliament, and common citizenship, was offered by Churchill as a way to keep France in the war with Germany. The idea was rapidly rejected by the French cabinet, leading to a change in the French government. In Britain, the idea drew on support for federalism, which was a progressive cause, but most politicians and diplomats were sceptical. Moreover, the Hankey Committee, appointed to consider the idea, correctly predicted problems over a host of issues, including tariffs, currency, the Commonwealth and sovereignty.[5] Led by Charles de Gaulle, the French who refused to co-operate with Germany took refuge in London, as did the fleeing governments of much of Europe.

Subsequently, Churchill proved ready to intervene with considerable force in Greece in order to prevent a Communist take-over in 1944–5. This readiness, which was taken forward by the post-war Labour government, looked back to the very bold approach he had taken during the Russian Civil War. Churchill's approach combined ideological commitment, a zeal for action, forward defence and imperial goals in a highly ambitious fashion that scarcely accorded with Britain's wider commitments in the aftermath of the First World War. Such over-stretch did not match the Toryism of restraint in the early eighteenth century, although it could be linked with the determination to fight on against France in 1797–1812 despite the collapse of the successive international coalitions of which Britain was a major part.

Thanks to Churchill and many of the renegades he brought to the fore, such as Anthony Eden, who became his Foreign Secretary (1940–5, 1951–5) and, in 1955–7, his successor as Prime Minister, the Conservative Party shed the 'Appeasement' label. This disguised the extent to which the party in the 1930s had been fully committed to a failed policy that had become a dirty hand in the 1950s. Labour proved more successful in avoiding the implications of the appeasing pacifism that had attracted its leaders, notably George Lansbury, in the early 1930s. Those who had condemned Appeasement were at the forefront of advocating the European option for Britain.

Churchill was to be given a reputation as a champion of European unity and federation, although this reputation is based on some extremely misleading and frequently misinterpreted remarks. In 1943, Churchill, in a broadcast, called for a 'Council of Europe' as part of the British propaganda offensive on German-occupied Europe. In his Zurich speech in September 1946, Churchill, then leader of the Conservative opposition, talked about the possibility of building 'a kind of United States of Europe', but he also made clear that the key element was a partnership between France and Germany, while Britain would act as the 'friend and sponsor' of such a scheme, rather than as a fully participating member. This was an aspiration Churchill repeated at The Hague in May 1948. At a 'United Europe' rally in 1947, Churchill declared that the international order rested on four principal pillars: the USA, the Soviet Union, the British empire and Commonwealth, and Europe.

Despite the portentous language, Churchill's commitment was always strictly qualified and more rhetorical than real, a point that was overlooked when he was cited in support of Remain views in the late 2010s. When he did clarify his position, as in May 1953 as Prime Minister, it was usually to suggest that Britain was with, not of, the European states. Churchill saw Britain's role as that of a benevolent sponsor and encouraging supporter rather than as a direct participant. He did not regard moves for Western European co-operation as a threat.

The 1950s

When the Conservatives, under Churchill, returned to power in October 1951, there was interest on their part in strengthening Western European defence, but far less so in any new Western European economic entity. Steel was to be privatised/denationalised by the Conservatives, not transferred to the control of a European organisation, the European Coal and Steel Community (ECSC). British political assumptions came first, with no sense that anything else was appropriate. In government from 1945 to 1951, Labour had refused to join negotiations for ECSC.

The British, both Labour and Conservative, preferred the American-led NATO solution for Western European security, although so did many Western Europeans. Nevertheless, active support, although, crucially, short of full membership, was also provided to the idea of a European Defence Community (EDC), which was seen as a way to control a rearmed Germany. The government only abandoned the European Army concept in June 1954 when its failure seemed certain: passed by the other five Parliaments of the ECSC, the measure had proved bitterly divisive in France, and was rejected by the French National Assembly that August.

The failure of the EDC did not prevent the process that led to the creation in 1958 of the very different European Economic Community (EEC), which, from 1967, was transformed into the European Community (EC) and, from 1982, into the European Union (EU). In the 1950s, there was no willingness, in France or Britain, to seek support from a popular referendum. This technique was employed in Europe in some cases, for example in Italy in 1946 as to whether to become a republic. It was not a British device, although it was used in Newfoundland to determine whether it should join Canada.

Had the EDC succeeded, it would have resulted in an important measure of European political integration which would have been led by defence, a field in which Britain played, and has continued to play, a major role; not the economic drive that was crucial in the development of the EEC. Conservatives might have found such a defence-based identity for Europe easier to accept. This counterfactual point serves as a reminder of the role of international contingencies in affecting domestic political options and responses. For instance, the 2013 German elections, by creating a need for Angela Merkel, the German Chancellor, to turn for support to the Social Democratic Party, made it less likely that Germany would support David Cameron's attempt to chart what he could present as a middle path on European policy.

During the 1950s, in Britain (as in France and Portugal) there was still a strong commitment to empire. Like its Labour predecessor, the Conservative government saw independence for India in 1947 as prefiguring not the end of empire but, rather, an international presence and identity based on its continuation, albeit more in the shape of informal control than hitherto. In the 1950s, British troops were to be used to fight for empire in Cyprus and Kenya, Malaya and Suez, followed in the 1960s by Aden. Indeed, despite the commitment, through NATO, to the defence of Western Europe, which led to the continued presence of British forces in West Germany after the end of post-war occupation, much of the British defence effort in the 1950s was dominated by concern about imperial security and that of allies outside Europe. This remained the case until the late 1960s.

France also evinced a firm commitment to empire. While keen on establishing NATO and ensuring American support for the defence of Western Europe, France devoted much military effort in the late 1940s and 1950s to trying to maintain its imperial position, first in Indochina and then in North Africa, in the end a debilitating and unsuccessful project. The French, however, proved far better than Britain at combining their imperial position with advancing their European interests, especially in the EEC. In part, this contrast reflected political circumstances and skill, but different political cultures were also significant.

British distance from the rest of Europe rested to a degree on a cultural separation, one, moreover, that was self-conscious. Whereas Benjamin Disraeli's Grand Tour to the East in 1830–1 helped renew his health, provided him with an understanding of his personal identity, and focused his political ideas and creative imagination,[6] there was no equivalent engagement with other cultures for British leaders in the 1950s. In 1951, when the Conservative politician Selwyn Lloyd became Minister of State at the Foreign Office, he admitted that he disliked foreigners, did not speak any foreign language, and, except for the Second World War, had never visited a foreign country. Lloyd went on to become Foreign Secretary in 1955–61. Holidays for many of those of Lloyd's interests were taken on Scottish grouse moors.

From a different social background, Harold Wilson, Labour leader from 1963 to 1976, took his holidays in the Scilly Isles. This was an admission of what was on his part a lack of sympathy for, indeed rejection of, cosmopolitan inclinations. Separately, if abroad meant the empire (including the dominions), it was an abroad understood in British terms.

This was also not solely an attitude of the 1950s. Nicholas Ridley noted that Margaret Thatcher, not a politician widely accused of cosmopolitanism, 'never attempted to speak in a foreign language', and she herself declared in January 1993 that 'the English language is soaked in values' that entailed political consequences. Jonathan Aitken joked that Thatcher thought that Sinai was the plural of sinus. Ridley himself claimed that English was very different from both French and German, being 'very clear and unambiguous'.[7] Roy Jenkins, a leading Labour politician who ended up as Deputy Head of the European Commission, was a prominent exception to this lack of cosmopolitanism at the level of most senior political figures in the 1960s–1980s. This cosmopolitanism was a matter not only of cultural style, but of political attitudes. There was also the element of the foreign perception of British politicians and their relative unwillingness to fit in with the norms of political conduct on the Continent.

There was a deeper reason, however, for distance between Britain and much of Western Europe. In Western Europe, many earlier political parties, especially those on the right, had been discredited by the events of the 1930s and 1940s, both Fascism and collaboration with German rule. These parties would be reborn, post-war, in the form of Christian Democracy, a tradition very different from that of British Conservatism. Christian Democracy was more corporatist and more ostentatiously concerned with social welfare, and also looked to roots in a Catholic political activism that was very different from that of the Conservative Party. In Germany, Christian Democracy was stronger in Catholic than Protestant areas, and remained so. The movement for Western European unity indeed owed much to the growth of Christian Democratic parties,[8] and the institutions founded as a result reflected their norms. Although the links are unclear and the influence uncertain, the Papacy consistently championed the movement. There was no comparable traction in Britain.

Across Europe, political structures had been found inadequate in the 1930s and 1940s. This inadequacy created a situation of political and governmental fluidity, and led to a sense that change was necessary. The establishment of the EEC indeed was part of a process in which the political structures and party politics of France, Germany and Italy were transformed between 1945 and 1958. For West Germany, multilateralism offered a way to recreate an acceptable German identity and to bind it to the West. Britain was separate from this process of transformation. She also lacked the direct experience of invasion, devastation and occupation that all the founder members of the EEC had recently suffered, although many British cities had been very heavily bombed.

The war left a British triumphalism which greatly affected identity and foreign policy priorities, notably over Europe, as well as influencing the way that the history of the first half of the century was interpreted in Britain. Victory was greeted as a British triumph, notwithstanding the massive disparity in military capabilities with Britain's American and Soviet allies. This response was the root of what Jean Monnet termed the 'illusion of victory', an illusion that led to the chronic over-extension of British power, its commitment to a high expenditure on the military, its struggle to produce a genuinely independent nuclear deterrent, and its continued efforts to 'punch above its weight' in international relations.

On the Continent, the disastrous experience of the Second World War, which, for France, was further underlined by the serious post-war military and political failures in Indochina and then, culminating in 1962, Algeria, lent energy to the idea of European union, and not least to the willingness, in return, to surrender some of the powers and prerogatives of the nation state to supranational bodies. In part this process was in order to provide an institutional constraint on political extremism, on the left or right, in any one country, but in part it was to avoid the possibility of a resumption of war among its members.

The EEC helped protect democracy in the member states, especially Italy, which was a British goal. Moreover, subsequent accessions to it were sometimes seen as ways to anchor democracy, as in Spain. Nevertheless, there was a deliberate democratic deficit built in as a structural part of the EEC and some of its founders, such as Monnet, were profoundly anti-democratic in outlook. This deficit remains the case today, whatever the language of accountability.

Such a process was easier for societies that were undergoing considerable centrally driven change, and whose political structures were being similarly transformed, than it was for Britain. Furthermore, this process also seemed less necessary for Britain. Despite the support of many pro-business Conservatives for entry into the EEC, there was a consistency in the distrust of some sections of the party for the nature of the entity being created. This was a distrust that Thatcher was to help shape in the 1980s, even though, at least in her treatment of local politics, she helped sustain the centralised character of British government. There was also a consistency in the distrust of some sections of the Labour Party for the EEC and what it was held to represent.

Those states defeated in the Second World War (Japan, Germany, France and Italy) experienced political and institutional change on the domestic and international level, while the victors (Britain, the USA and the Soviet Union) essentially maintained their political structures. The changes that came in Britain were very much one-nation ones, for the Labour governments of 1945–51 were not greatly concerned to spread their model on the Continent. Indeed, British Socialist idealism was generally directed towards the Commonwealth, particularly India, and the empire, and focused on post-independence arrangements. In part this emphasis reflected distance from the Communists who were prominent in Western Europe, notably France and Italy, and who posed the possibility of 'popular front' governments there. The Labour government very much adopted an anti-Communist line: in Britain, its empire, Western Europe and more generally.

On 9 November 1954, Churchill, still Prime Minister, declared at the Lord Mayor's Banquet in London that Britain was 'developing increasingly intimate ties with France, Germany, Italy, and the Low Countries which are stronger and more practical than any that have yet been devised'. However, in political and institutional terms, the establishment of the EEC on 1 January 1958, as a result of the Messina conferences of 1955 and 1956 and the Treaty of Rome of 1957, was both effect and cause of a major divergence between Britain and the leading Western European states. French policy, focused on the establishment of the EEC, was cemented by West German willingness to accept the concessions France required. In part, the EEC represented a way for France to anchor West Germany and thus, in response to the experience of German invasions going back to 1792, overcome the parameters of history in terms of fear and hatred. The six original members of the EEC were France, Italy, Belgium, Luxembourg, the Netherlands and West Germany. They were the Continental members of the European Defence Community.

The divergence between Britain and the EEC was taken further in 1959 when the British Conservative government, now under Harold Macmillan, Prime Minister from 1957 to 1963, inspired a European Free Trade Association (EFTA) of countries not in the EEC, including Austria, Denmark, Norway, Portugal,

Sweden and Switzerland. Subsequently, Britain was to make a free trade agreement with Ireland. Reflecting very much the instrumentalist nature of policy, EFTA was deliberately restricted to commercial matters. It lacked any location in a historical narrative, let alone the idealistic and federalist flavour of the EEC: the Treaty of Rome had pledged to work for 'an ever closer union of the peoples of Europe'. Indeed, although essentially quiet, there is a distinct strand linking EFTA and Britain's policy at the time to attitudes still expressed today. EFTA did not represent opposition to Europe but, instead, a different type of European identity, one rejected by the six who formed the EEC. A British working party on the Common Market in October 1955 had concluded that a successful EEC would be bad for Britain and, if possible, should be frustrated. In diplomatic terms, the main purpose of the 'outer seven' in EFTA was to undermine the cohesion of the 'inner six' in the EEC by offering a looser structure within a free trade area confined only to industrial goods. This was an arrangement believed to be more attractive to West Germany and the Benelux countries than the high tariff barrier around the EEC's customs union. Such an arrangement would also not threaten Commonwealth trade in food products or the British system of agricultural subsidy.

EFTA was established by a Conservative government, and reflected the degree to which British policymakers (in response to Continental counterparts doing the same) pressed for a form of European integration that matched their assumptions and that was designed to serve British interests. The existence and goals of EFTA were intended as a clear constraint on the possibility that the EEC would serve as the basis of a supranational Europe. Nevertheless, such hopes of EFTA were rapidly dispelled and, within months, Macmillan's government began the process of bridge-building with the EEC as it woke up to a number of painful economic, diplomatic and defence realities. Too much attention had been devoted to global diplomacy and imperial issues rather than the realities of the emerging situation in Western Europe.

The sense of Britain's distance from the Continent was eroded by the wholesale retreat from empire down to 1964, a process that greatly speeded up after 1957 when Macmillan succeeded Eden as Prime Minister. Empire had been presented, notably in the eighteenth and nineteenth centuries, as a stage to a process of linked development, a civilisational model that ultimately looked back to the idea of Britain as a modern Rome. However, under Macmillan, this abandonment of empire was increasingly accompanied by a view that the Commonwealth, as most of the former empire had become, would not, in practice, be able to meet or, indeed, contribute greatly to Britain's economic, political or security needs, a view that was to be fully justified by subsequent events. The Commonwealth has never acted as an effective alternative to Britain's European identity and interests, and this despite suggestions in the late 2010s of such a possibility. EFTA proved, like the Commonwealth, a structure that did not, and could not, fulfil the hopes placed upon it. At the same time, disappointment has not prevented many other structures from working, including the UN and the EEC.

Some traditional Conservative interests, such as the military and those linked to white settlers in the colonies, led to concern about empire.[9] There was to be serious division over Southern Rhodesia following its unilateral declaration of independence in 1965. However, this concern was less the case with much of the party's middle-class support, which was increasingly prominent in constituency associations and at party conferences. Leaders such as Edward Heath and Reginald Maudling (who became Colonial Secretary in 1961), neither of whom came from the traditional ruling group, felt little commitment to the empire. Conservative disengagement from empire was also related to 'new' Commonwealth immigration and to the empire 'coming home' in ways which certain politicians (and some of their constituents) found distinctly troubling.

The balance between the generations was also important, with the young certainly not experiencing the sense of discontinuity felt by their elders. Generational shifts also related to specific points, for example attitudes to British settlers in Africa. The empire, moreover, served as a foil for defining the British national character. Commitment to empire was increasingly perceived as the antithesis of what is meant to be 'modern', as an obstacle to economic reform, an emblem of outdated social values, and a view out of kilter with 'democratic' political values. It appeared redundant.

The same may well be the case with differing generational attitudes at present toward Brexit. That is less clear, however, notably because the issues are more urgent and also because the loss of sovereignty represented by membership in the EU is not an issue, like empire, that recedes.

Trying to Join the EEC

Support for joining the EEC became more widespread in British political circles as it became clear that the organisation would be more than a short-term flurry; indeed, that it would be a success in terms of the level of economic growth enjoyed by the member states. Thus, the impact of the short term was, again, important. Western European growth rates were high, although this situation was not largely due to the EEC. In part, this growth reflected recovery from wartime damage, the sensible investment of American Marshall Plan Aid, and also the possibility of making rapid industrial advances by introducing American manufacturing and organisational techniques. Structural reforms were also important. In agriculture, mechanisation led to a movement of workers from the land, especially in France and Germany, into more productive sectors, and, therefore, to an increase in per capita productivity. Trade liberalisation also helped greatly. The EEC took the credit for economic growth, although much, in fact, was due to the cutting of tariffs following the General Agreement on Tariffs and Trade (GATT). Signed in 1947, GATT was a key aspect of the remaking of the world economic order in a more liberal direction by the USA, as American policymakers sought to avoid what they saw as a mistaken isolationism after the First World War and, instead, to shape a strong non-Communist West, an attitude that lasted until the Trump administration.

Similarly, especially down to 1970 but also thereafter, NATO and, in particular, the American military commitment to Western Europe were more important to peace within this region, let alone its security, than anything provided by the EEC, although protagonists of the EEC were to claim the credit. As a result, the EEC was scarcely of central consequence to those Conservatives who were primarily concerned about defence. In a major shift from historical tradition, however, they had to reconceptualise ideas about defence, not least as empire ebbed, around the American alliance and the defence of Western Europe: new partnerships and new commitments. The Cold War and the pressing fear of a Soviet invasion of Western Europe were major influences on the foreign and defence policies of Britain and Western European countries. They provided a key convergence of purpose although not a unity of one.

Alongside defence, the international economic context appeared to be of increasing note, a situation that reflected problems with the British economy as well as concern about trends. In the first fifteen years of the EEC, West Germany had an average annual growth rate of 5 per cent and overtook Britain as the strongest West European economy. France had an average annual growth rate of 5.5 per cent. Italian industrial exports also boomed. EFTA, in contrast, was a relative failure. Influenced by liberal-minded economists, the West German government adopted pro-competition policies and fostered currency stability, although, until it adopted the Godesberg Programme in 1959, the SPD (Social Democratic) opposition favoured state planning. More generally, the West German economic and financial system contrasted with the nationalisations and state control seen in France and Britain, let alone Communist East Germany, to which the West German concept of the social market was deliberately a rival model. As Economics Minister, Ludwig Erhard was sympathetic to the British idea of an International Free Trade Area (FTA), proposed by the Conservative government in 1957, but Charles de Gaulle persuaded Konrad Adenauer, the West German Chancellor, to overrule Erhard and reject the proposal. The FTA answered British goals, not only in that the focus was on free trade, but also because Britain would have played an equal role in its formation rather than having to join the already established EEC.

The loss of British influence in Washington was also an issue, as America was keen for Britain to join the EEC. This was an aspect of the long-term American strategy to end or at least weaken the British empire and, more specifically, to move Britain from imperial power to the supporter of, indeed voice for, American interests in Europe, a strategy that repeatedly posed problems for British politicians. The British had earlier assumed that the United States would be happy to co-operate with Britain separately and closely, but this proved unfounded. The year 1959 saw the first bilateral meeting of American and Soviet leaders, showing that Britain could be left out. In a very different context, there was an instructive parallel with strong anxieties linked to the Trump-Putin summit in 2018.

After the failure of the FTA, Macmillan applied to join the EEC in 1961, in part because he thought the Americans wanted a stronger Western Europe, as indeed they did. He feared that otherwise he would have less influence with the United States, and therefore be less able to win American support for British interests elsewhere in the world and for the transformation of the British nuclear deterrent. Competition with France was also involved. President Kennedy indeed pressed Macmillan to join the EEC because he (correctly) feared that de Gaulle had ambitions to lead a Europe separate from American interests, and that the EEC might prove the basis for this 'Third Force'.

Thus, a role in the EEC was increasingly seen as crucial to Britain's international influence.[10] If this stance, part of the continued primacy of foreign policy, was an aspect of the established practice of trying to run a European policy that would serve Britain's wider interests, the context was now very different. The American stance on Britain's position is an issue that has affected British policy within Europe ever since. Successive Prime Ministers have been overly impressed by American views on the matter. Most famously, as represented by the oft-repeated remark about Europe lacking a single phone number, a comment associated with Henry Kissinger, President Nixon's National Security Adviser, later Secretary of State, the thrust of the policy is for an end to national distinctiveness, indeed a sort of tidying-up exercise. Furthermore, particularly in the 1950s, the United States was willing to encourage Franco-West German reconciliation as an aspect of a necessary European self-reliance. However, this reconciliation was to harm British interests and, in the end, to challenge those of the United States, especially once, but even before, the Soviet threat had ended. Trump's anger with Germany in 2018 looked back to the consequences of this situation.

Macmillan's application to join the EEC paralleled his policies of disengagement from empire and was also linked to attempts at internal economic management. Having won the 1959 general election, in part as a result of a self-conscious consumerism deliberately fuelled by cuts in taxation and interest rates, Macmillan found, by 1961, that the economy was hitting major problems, with a rising trade gap—the balance of payments and its pressure on the value of sterling, as well as higher wage costs, and an unsuccessful attempt to control wages. With the Conservative record for economic management under pressure, Macmillan, a corporatist who had called in the 1930s for state intervention, a policy different from that of the Conservative mainstream of that period, now showed support for government economic planning, which was presented as the way to ensure modernisation. This was an important aspect of his rejection of the earlier policies of Conservative governments, seen also, for example, in his rush to part with empire and also in his break with the Treasury team over public spending in 1958. In 1961, there was backing from Macmillan for French-style 'indicative' planning; indeed, France in the 1960s benefited from economic growth and restructuring and from an ability to control inflation.

In Britain, this aspiration led, in 1962, to the establishment of 'Neddy', the National Economic Development Council, with its task of creating a national economic plan, and its membership drawn from employers, trade unions and government. Macmillan's call for a 'new approach' included not only more planning and better labour relations, but also entry into the EEC.[11] This was a response to the real and apparent weaknesses of the British economy, which the levels of growth existing within the EEC made more dramatic, a response that did not accord with earlier ideas of renewal through imperial preference. Yet again, relations with the Continent made greater sense within a context of domestic political issues, a situation that continues to the present and that is highly relevant for the Brexit debate in recent years.

The entire policy failed. The National Incomes Commission, which Macmillan saw as the arbitrator of incomes policy, was boycotted by the unions, 'Neddy' had no real effect on policy, and in June 1962 de Gaulle made it clear to Macmillan that he preferred an EEC without Britain, telling him that British entry would totally alter the character of the EEC in political as well as economic terms, and that Britain was too close to America. The last appeared underlined when Macmillan opted for American Polaris missiles as the way to deliver British nuclear warheads.

In contrast, de Gaulle actively pursued reconciliation with West Germany, then under a Christian Democratic government, not least on his visit there in September 1962. This led to the Elysée Treaty between France and West Germany in January 1963. Adenauer had moved towards de Gaulle and away from Britain and the USA in 1961, in part because he was concerned that the latter were insufficiently resolute over the future of Berlin and over other West German issues with the Soviet Union. The link with France remained the alignment of West German policy until Adenauer retired in 1963 and was replaced by Erhard. In return for the political weight West Germany thus gained from French support, the West German government was willing to make economic concessions to France and to accept the French verdict on Britain. This prefigured the closeness between the two powers, not least in opposition to Britain, during the Mitterrand–Kohl and Chirac–Schröder partnerships from the 1980s to the 2000s, a closeness Macron has struggled to establish with the less emollient Merkel.

As an instance of the role of contingency, once Erhard gained power in 1963, West German policy then shifted towards Britain and the USA, hitting relations with France. Had this been the policy earlier, then de Gaulle would have been under greater pressure over the British application. However, an inability to affect the nature of relations between France and West Germany greatly limited British options, whichever political party was in power in London.

To de Gaulle, the nation state, at least the French state, and therefore French interests within the EEC, came first, and this attitude affected his policy towards the EEC and Britain. On 14 January 1963, notwithstanding the support for British entry from the other five members of the EEC, France vetoed the British application, de Gaulle declaring at a press conference at the Elysée Palace, 'England is insular ... the nature and structure and economic context of England differs profoundly from those of the other states of the Continent'.[12] Britain would also have challenged French interest in developing EEC defence and foreign policies, and its shaping of the EEC's agricultural policy.

A more general difference between the political cultures in the two countries had been demonstrated in October 1962 when Georges Pompidou, whom de Gaulle had appointed as Prime Minister that April, was immediately reappointed after his defeat on a motion of no confidence in the Chamber of Deputies had led to his resignation. De Gaulle's attitudes reflected at once an autocratic manner that helped foster a serious democratic deficit, and a rejection of the political culture and structure of the earlier Fourth Republic, a rejection that was deliberately intended to achieve this more authoritarian goal.

The French veto dampened the debate within Britain. There, although there was a degree of proto-Euroscepticism in the Conservative Party, particularly among those who criticised Macmillan's views,[13] it was Labour, then in opposition, that was more ambivalent about membership. In part, this ambivalence reflected the traditional economic protectionism that had led to opposition in Britain to free trade in the 1900s, the grand 'project' for national and imperial renewal of the Edwardian age. In the 1960s, there was a fear that Continental workers would accept lower levels of social protection and welfare, and thus price their British counterparts out of work. This anxiety prefigured concerns in the 2000s and 2010s about the impact of EU enlargement in the shape of Eastern European workers providing serious competition both by migrating to Western Europe and by producing cheaper goods in Eastern Europe. Jeremy Corbyn, Labour's leader from 2015, seeks to offer a revival of this one-nation renewal, and it provides a particular slant on his otherwise pronounced internationalism.

There was also a sense of national identity under threat. This sense was memorably captured by Hugh Gaitskell, the leader of the Labour Party, who declared, in a television interview on 21 September 1962, that entry into the EEC 'means the end of Britain as an independent nation; we become no more than Texas or California in the United States of Europe. It means the end of a thousand years of history.' Gaitskell's history was a bit dodgy: Britain had only existed as a state since 1707, and England had been conquered by Danes (1013–16) and Normans (1066) in the eleventh century. However, Gaitskell struck a note of Labour patriotism that had earlier affected figures such as Clement Attlee and Ernest Bevin, and was to be seen anew with Peter Shore and Tony Benn. This contrasted with a Labour internationalist tradition that in some respects emerged anew under Tony Blair (leader 1994–2007) and Ed Miliband (leader 2010–15), albeit conspicuously lacking the strand of international workers' solidarity.

For Gaitskell, wartime memories of the Commonwealth supporting Britain meant a lot. He declared that he would not sell 'the Commonwealth down the river' and, with reference to the First World War, that 'We, at least do not intend to forget Vimy Ridge and Gallipoli', battles in which dominion forces, respectively Canadian and Anzac (Australian and New Zealand), had played a major role. These were memories that had meaning for Attlee and Bevin, and drew on ideas of a shared kinship that also had meaning on the right.[14] Gaitskell had, moreover, been much affected by the unanimous hostility to British entry expressed at a meeting of Commonwealth Socialist leaders that he called in late 1962.

After Labour, under Gaitskell's successor (from 1963), Harold Wilson, came to power as a result of the general election of October 1964, there was an attempt to maintain Britain as an international power (while also using planning to transform the economy), an attempt which indicated a strong confidence in national remedies. This approach was in line with the instinctual sympathies of many Conservatives. Labour's policies, however, lacked a sound economic basis, not least because of an overvalued currency, acute balance-of-payments problems, and low industrial productivity, which were compounded by labour militancy and political mismanagement. These problems forced the government to abandon its political and military prospectus and, in November 1967, in a humiliating fashion, its defence of sterling, which was devalued by 14.3 per cent.

The failure of an independent economic, political and international strategy encouraged a focus on Europe. Discarding remaining 'east of Suez' imperial commitments, commitments that had a strong resonance in British history back into the seventeenth century, defence priorities, instead, were focused on deterring a Soviet invasion of Western Europe. In May 1967, Wilson launched a new bid to join the EEC, securing a massive House of Commons pro-entry vote of 488 to 62, although public opinion was not that clear-cut.[15]

Having put entry into their 1966 election manifesto, the Conservative Party was in no position to complain, although many individual Conservatives did so. Moreover, the populist nationalism that was to be offered and defined anew by Enoch Powell, when he began to attack the consequences of immigration in April 1968, was unacceptable to the party leader, Heath. Distrustful of Powell and conspicuously lacking charisma or the ability to strike an effective patriotic note, Heath was no populist. He was to prove an ardent supporter of EEC membership.

Like Macmillan, Wilson was motivated by a sense of the need to redress declining international influence, not least due to the realisation that bases east of Suez, particularly Aden and Singapore, could no longer be maintained. Wilson was also motivated by commercial considerations, notably the higher growth rates in the EEC. Unlike Gaitskell, he and the successive Labour Foreign Secretaries, George Brown and Michael Stewart, were resolved on taking Britain 'into Europe'. Some of their colleagues, such as Jenkins, later a pivotal figure in the EEC and, subsequently, an inspiration to Blair (pressing him hard, once Prime Minister, to adopt the euro), were more enthusiastic about what they regarded as the political options and possibilities stemming from a greater British role within Europe. Like Heath, Jenkins scorned populism. His attitudes in social policy as Home Secretary reflected a contempt for majority views.

Whatever the motive, there was more British political support for entry than there had been in 1961–3. De Gaulle, however, in November 1967 again blocked entry, this time emphasising the underlying weakness of the British economy, which was very apparent at that point. A keen geopolitician, happy to think in terms of rival political blocs, de Gaulle argued that Britain was driven to seek membership because of a sense of vulnerability, and on 27 November 1967 he declared that the British people

doubtless see more and more clearly that in face of the great movements which are now sweeping the world—the huge power of the United States, the growing power of the Soviet Union, the renascent power of the Continental countries of Europe, the newly emerging power of China—its own structures, its traditions, its activities and even its national character are from now on all at risk. This is brought home to her, day after day, by the grave economic, financial and currency problems with which she is currently contending. This is why she feels the profound need to find some sort of framework, even a European one if need be, which would enable her to safeguard her own identity, to play a leading role, and at the same time, to lighten some of her burden.[16]

This geopolitical approach reflected a continent-based spatial imagination that downplayed the value of maritime links and oceanic identities, particularly in the North Atlantic, as well as underplaying the real and potential roles of the flow of trade and capital. As such, the approach was in line with the dominant historical strand in French strategic culture, one that was different from that of Britain.

When negotiations resumed, there was a different President in France and a new Prime Minister in Britain. De Gaulle's resignation in 1969, after the French government had lost a referendum on constitutional changes, was a necessary prelude to the invitation by the EEC in 1970 to four applicants—Britain, Ireland, Denmark and Norway—to resume negotiations, Britain being the key negotiating partner. De Gaulle's successor, Pompidou, President from 1969 until his early death in 1974, was concerned about growing West German strength and the need to balance it, and not by the challenge from Anglo-American links. He was also more committed to the EEC than de Gaulle had been, and therefore more willing to respond to his partners' pressure for enlargement.

By the time serious negotiations resumed, at the end of June 1970, Heath had replaced Wilson: the latter lost office on 18 June in a surprise general election result, twelve days before the beginning of negotiations. The work done by the Wilson government, however, was important, not least because its official team, negotiating briefs and timetable were all used by its successor. This instance of continuity underlines the danger of assuming that party distinctions are necessarily always the key element.

Heath had been the chief negotiator in the application vetoed by France in 1963. As Prime Minister, pushing hard for membership, which he saw as crucial to the modernisation of Britain, Heath was also keen on a new geopolitical alignment. He was not eager for close co-operation with the USA, particularly under President Nixon, whose policies had led to American intervention in Cambodia in 1970. Furthermore, Heath was determined not to be branded as the American spokesman in Europe. To Heath, Europe represented a welcome alternative to the USA. He was later to be hostile to Thatcher's focus on Anglo-American links.[17]

Heath also saw membership as crucial to the revival of Britain's economic fortunes. Specifically, he regarded membership as likely to lead to an economic competition that would ensure reform and greater efficiency in Britain, prefiguring the view that John Major was to take when pressing, as Chancellor of the Exchequer, for joining the ERM (Exchange Rate Mechanism), as Britain did in October 1990, even at a disadvantageous rate. In both cases, this was to be foolish economics and bad politics. Heath's views on the economic benefits of membership accorded with his emphasis on and view of modernisation, the theme he pushed in the 1970 election campaign. However, joining the EEC would be far more disruptive for Britain than it was for the original member states, because their trade was overwhelmingly Eurocentric, while, in contrast, less than half of Britain's trade was within Europe, although that trade was increasing.

As with Macmillan and Wilson, a lack of confidence in national solutions led to modernisation being focused on the EEC. To Heath, Europe was the modern alternative to an anachronistic emphasis on global influence and to a naive confidence in the Commonwealth. Instead, he saw both prosperity and security as answered by European co-operation. The 'pooling of sovereignty' and the creation of supranational European institutions did not worry Heath, because he felt that a reformed and revitalised Britain would be able to play a major role in leading the EEC and shaping its policy. Indeed, Heath and many other Conservatives denied that the country would compromise its independence or sovereignty.

The negotiations were relatively easy for two reasons. First, Heath was prepared to surrender much in order to obtain membership. As a state seeking membership, Britain anyway negotiated from weakness, but Heath seriously accentuated this, badly neglecting national interests. Heath accepted the EEC's expensive, inefficient and protectionist Common Agricultural Policy (CAP), despite the fact that it had little to offer Britain, although he had scant choice. The CAP has ensured that the financial consequences of membership have repeatedly not served British interests. Indeed, Thatcher's subsequent obduracy over the rebate on the British contribution to the EEC was forced on her by Heath, who, characteristically, did not offer her any support over the issue.

The resulting agricultural subsidies and higher food costs of the CAP replaced cheap food imports from the Commonwealth, particularly New Zealand lamb. They, indeed, had to be excluded to maintain the market for Continental products, while rising food prices fed through into the already serious problem of inflation within Britain. Entry into the EEC also led to a loss of national control over nearby fishing grounds, an issue that was of great importance to the fishing communities concerned.

Negotiations were successfully concluded in July 1971. Ignoring difficulties raised by ministers, Heath pushed membership hard on its economic merits, arguing that it opened up markets, and the White Paper claimed that Britain would be able to influence policy from being in the centre of Europe. In contrast, Heath said little about possible political consequences. He declared in the House of Commons that there would be no lessening of 'national identity or an erosion of essential national sovereignty' and, on television, that 'a country's vital interest cannot be overruled'. Heath ignored clear warnings to the contrary.

Secondly, negotiations were relatively easy because there was only limited opposition within the Conservative Party, still less the government. The Commons voted in favour of entry by 356 to 244 on 28 October 1971. Heath had reluctantly conceded a free vote, the course he had initially rejected, but that was urged by his Chief Whip, Francis Pym, in order to help win over Labour support, which was weaker than it had been under the Wilson government. Entry was criticised most strongly by the powerful left wing of the Labour Party.[18] This opposition helped lead Wilson to declare that, while he was unwilling to reject British entry in principle, he opposed entry on the terms which Heath had negotiated, a policy that anticipated that of Jeremy Corbyn towards Brexit. Wilson was also opposed to the CAP, which he correctly saw as a serious burden for Britain.

Labour supporters of EEC entry, led by Jenkins, however, were willing to defy a three-line whip, and to vote with the government, thus providing a secure parliamentary majority for entry, and one able to overcome both the bulk of the Labour Party and the role of any Conservative rebels. Although 39 Conservative MPs voted against, 69 Labour MPs were willing to vote in favour, while 20 abstained. As at the present moment, the major parliamentary parties were divided.

The Common Market Membership Treaty was signed at Brussels on 22 January 1972, and on 1 January 1973 it took effect. Britain became a full member of the European Economic Community, the European Atomic Energy Community, and the European Coal and Steel Community. Very much following the British line, Denmark and Ireland joined on the same day, but Norway found the Common Fisheries Policy unacceptable. Large majorities against entry in public opinion polls in Britain were ignored, as were the referenda in four constituencies held in August 1971. This was, more generally, a pattern in the politics of the period. There was a hostility among Conservatives to referenda-style government.

1974–1990

EEC membership was re-examined after Labour returned to power under Wilson in February 1974, in large part in an effort to quieten critics on the Labour left. Far from displaying a principled commitment to a European cause, the divided Labour government entered into a protracted and largely cosmetic renegotiation of Britain's terms of entry, which brought some regional aid, of value mostly to Labour constituencies, and which allowed the continued import of some Commonwealth foodstuffs. The fundamentals, however, were not changed. The 1972 European Communities Act, which gave EEC law primacy over British law, was not altered, the CAP was not reformed, insufficient thought was given to Britain's likely contribution level to the EEC budget, and the Commonwealth trading system was irreparably weakened. The renegotiated terms were passed in the Commons on 9 April 1975. Nevertheless, the governing Labour party was far more opposed than the Conservatives, and the support of the latter was needed in order to get the measure through. In the end, 145 Labour MPs and 8 Conservatives voted against the Bill, and 137 Labour and 249 Conservatives in favour. This reflected a Conservative parliamentary party that was very much in favour of the EEC.

To surmount party divisions, Wilson then launched a constitutional novelty: a referendum campaign on Britain's continued membership of the EEC. So that supporters and opponents could both campaign, the principle of collective cabinet responsibility did not apply in the referendum, which was held on 5 June 1975. According to the results, 67.2 per cent of those who voted (about 65 per cent of the electorate; a smaller percentage than in 2016) favoured membership, the only areas showing a majority against being the Shetlands and the Western Isles (of Scotland). In 2016, support was much more finely balanced, both in the overall result and as far as the constituent parts of the United Kingdom were concerned.

The available evidence suggests that public opinion was very volatile on the EEC, implying a lack of interest or understanding, and that the voters tended to follow the advice of the party leaderships, all of which supported continued membership. The opposition was stigmatised as extreme, although it was from across the political spectrum, from Powell on the nationalist right to Tony Benn on the left. Benn's objection was that the EEC was undemocratic and could not be got rid of, which was his litmus test of a democracy. A vigil was held by Churchill's statue in Parliament Square. Britain stayed in.

As a consequence of the referendum, relations with the EEC were not to become as divisive a political issue again until they emerged in the late 1980s as the focus for the ultimately fatal split within the Thatcher government. The anti-EEC movement itself largely disappeared from sight after 1975.[19]

At the same time, the pace of European unification was modest, and Britain was certainly not at the forefront. There was no real controversy in 1979 when, fearful of the deflationary consequences of tying sterling to a strong Deutschmark, the Labour government under Jim Callaghan decided not to join the ERM, the only one of the nine EEC states not to do so. This was symptomatic of the reluctant Europeanism of the Callaghan government (1976–9), which, in turn, reflected Callaghan's ingrained Atlanticism. In the light of subsequent developments, it is ironic that Thatcher criticised the decision not to enter the ERM, which, indeed, was regarded by some as the basis for monetary and economic union.

Under Thatcher, Conservative leader from 1975 to 1990, and Prime Minister from 1979 to 1990, EEC issues took no real role in the 1979, 1983 and 1987 general election campaigns; and it is possible to read accounts of them in which the EEC scarcely appears.[20] In contrast, the 1982 Falklands War played a major role in the 1983 general election. In part because European integration did not then gather pace, the anti-EEC movement remained weak in the 1980s until it revived late in the decade.

An instance of the complacency of this period is provided by the autobiography of Denis Healey, a prominent Labour politician of the 1970s, which was published in 1989. He devoted very little space to the 1975 referendum, described as an issue 'marginal to our real problems', which, indeed, were dominated by pressing fiscal and economic issues; while, of the direct elections to the European Parliament, Healey remarked:

> Many of my colleagues feared that direct elections would give the so-called Euro-MPs the political authority to assume powers to override the British Parliament. In fact, as I predicted at the time, the Euro-MPs now have less influence on events than before. Elected by a small proportion of the electorate from very large constituencies, they lack political authority; and because they are cut off from their national parliaments they lack influence where it really matters.[21]

Matters became far more divisive during the later Thatcher years. Again, this development was linked to domestic divisions, although this linkage had not been much in evidence earlier, as, for example, in 1984 when the rebate reduced the net amount of Britain's overall subsidy to the EEC through the disproportionate payments Britain was making.

A lack of acute domestic division was also the case when the Single European Act was signed in 1986. This Act was designed to give effect to the programme for an internal market launched the previous year. Such a policy of free trade seemed in accord with British views, and Thatcher had pressed for the opening of markets in order to encourage competition. However, the increase in EEC powers required to oversee the market was more of a problem in the long term and should have been anticipated and guarded against. In enforcing open markets, the EEC also proved open to political horse-trading that did not suit the British. Furthermore, the internal market represented a major restriction of the role of individual states, and thus of the position and functions of government and Parliament. In addition, the Single European Market did not lead to the promised economic transformation. In practice, the Delors report on competitiveness and growth, unintentionally, aggravated structural economic problems in the EEC.

Keen on free trade and a vocal advocate of economic liberalisation, Thatcher was critical of what she saw as a preference for economic controls and centralist planning in the EEC. Both became more marked in the late 1980s as a major attempt was made to energise the EEC. This attempt owed much to French Socialists, particularly Jacques Delors, President of the EEC Commission from 1985 to 1994, and reflected their response to the problems of executing their policies within France itself earlier in the decade: Delors had been François Mitterrand's Minister of Economics and Finance. During the Giscard d'Estaing presidency (1974–81), the conservative Barre government (1976–81) had pursued economic liberalisation, cutting the government's role and emphasising market forces, that was in line with Thatcherite assumptions, not least in putting the control of inflation above the fight with unemployment, but these policies were dramatically reversed in 1981 after the Socialist candidate, Mitterrand, won the presidential election.

In many respects, the policies that subsequently followed in France in 1981–3 linked the traditional nostrums of the left and of state control and intervention with the aspirations for regulation and social management that underlie aspects of the modern European project. Reflation focused less on modernisation than on support for traditional constituencies (coal, steel and shipbuilding in France in the early 1980s, agriculture today), while a determined attempt was made to control manufacturing and the financial system. Taxation in France in 1981–3 was directed toward redistribution, with a wealth tax matched by an increase in the minimum wage and by a cut in the working week.

This French experience rested in part on a refusal to accept the disciplines posed by international economic competition and, indeed, on their rejection as alien Anglo-American concepts. Mitterrand's ambitious policies, however, had rapidly been thwarted by economic realities, with the policies reversed in 1983. To French politicians, Europe seemed not so much an alternative as a way to give effect to their thwarted visions. In 1985, Delors became President of the European Commission and he revived the policy of European integration, seeing it as a complement to the enlargement of the 'nine' to the 'twelve': Greece joined in 1981, and Spain and Portugal in 1986. To Delors, a stronger Commission and a weaker national veto were crucial if progress was to be made; indeed, he used the Commission to provide a driving force for integration. This was a position it lost in the early and mid-2000s, as national governments came to play a more active role in the EU, only for the financial crisis of the late 2000s to evoke new calls for unification. The energy of the French left was strengthened in 1988 when Mitterrand was re-elected as President. Mitterrand's success put Thatcher in a vulnerable position.

France's ambitions for the EEC were accentuated when German unification became an option after the fall of the Berlin Wall in 1989. Deeper European integration seemed a way to contain Germany, just as the original establishment of the EEC had been regarded as a way to anchor West Germany. French ambitions for social policy helped ensure that Labour abandoned its essentially anti-EEC position and, instead, became the more pro-European of the two main British political parties.

With her own views sustained by an awareness of the vocal anti-European lobby,[22] Thatcher had no time for the integrationist ambitions pushed by Delors. She correctly discerned their serious implications for Britain and, indeed, Europe. In September 1988, Thatcher declared at the opening ceremony of the 39th academic year of the College of Europe in Bruges: 'We have not successfully rolled back the frontiers of the state in

Britain, only to see them re-imposed at a European level, with a European super-state exercising a new dominance from Brussels.' Indeed, Thatcher could point to the pursuit at the national level of her own economic policies as leading to economic revival.

Thatcher felt closer to Ronald Reagan, the American President from 1981 to 1989, whom she had recognised as a fellow spirit when they first met in 1975, than to European leaders, such as Giscard d'Estaing, Mitterrand and Helmut Kohl, German Chancellor from 1982 to 1998. Their patronising manner was not suited to managing her assertiveness. Thatcher's government was also more influenced than its Continental counterparts by the emergence of neo-liberal free-market economics in the 1980s, particularly in the USA. This influence reflected not only Thatcher's Americanism, her commitment to Britain becoming an enterprising society and dynamic economy on the American model, but also the greater hostility of much of the Conservative Party to the corporatist and regulatory state, certainly as compared with the attitude of the Continental Christian Democrats, let alone their Socialist counterparts.

This situation was accentuated by the exigencies of coalition systems on the Continent, for systems of proportional representation are generally less subject to new political departures, or, if so, are so as a result of changes in which the electorate often plays only a limited role. Kohl's Christian Democrats gained power in 1982 because the Free Democrats switched to them, whereas Thatcher had become Prime Minister in 1979 because voters' preferences had changed. For Thatcher, the USA, not Europe, was the entity that could or would provide the military and political requirements of security for Britain and leadership for the West.[23]

Thatcher met the challenges of the passing of empire, the Cold War, Americanisation and the European Community by combining an assertion of national resolve with her status as the figurehead for the market economy, which had an international significance and sweep. This gave her a means of promoting economic modernisation that was compatible both with traditional free trade priorities and with the importance of the nation state. The Cold War, rather than the empire, a more historic entity and traditional identity, served her as the basis for a foreign policy that still asserted a national role, in a way that her successors were unable to imitate because the context had changed.

Thatcher's own attitude towards the EEC was more bluntly put by Nicholas Ridley, a minister close to her, who was forced to resign from the cabinet after telling the editor of *The Spectator* in July 1990 that the European Community was a 'German racket designed to take over the whole of Europe'. Bernard Ingram, formerly Thatcher's press secretary and very much 'his mistress's voice', referred to the EEC in 1992 as a 'Franco-German ramp'.[24]

Thatcher's alienation became more serious as the EEC developed in a more ambitious direction. She was also unhappy about the unification of Germany in 1990, fearing that this would lead to an overly powerful and assertive Germany. To France, Germany had to be anchored in the EEC, to Britain in NATO, but unification made NATO a less potent context for German policymaking. Much of the British government and civil service, including Douglas Hurd, who became Foreign Secretary in 1989, did not share Thatcher's doubts and, instead, actively supported unification. Hurd thought Thatcher's use of history, notably her references to the Second World War, ahistorical.[25]

By supporting the European Communities (Amendment) Act approving the Single European Act in 1986, and thus legally joining the domestic market to the EEC, Thatcher had, while encouraging the single market, given new powers to the European Parliament and abolished the veto rights of a single state in some key areas of decision-making; but, with key bits of information withheld from her, she no more realised what would flow from this, as the momentum for the creation of a 'single market' gathered pace, than she understood the consequences of her failure to retain support among Conservative backbenchers. As a politician, Thatcher was gravely weakened by her inability to appreciate the potential strength of those she despised. She did not support holding a referendum over EEC membership. Indeed, she would have seen such a solution as a distraction from government policy and as an unnecessary limitation of parliamentary authority.

Thatcher fell out with key members of her cabinet, including former supporters, over what, partly as a result, became the crucial issue of Europe, notably with the Foreign Secretary, the pro-European Geoffrey Howe, over joining the ERM. This constituted stage one of a projected economic and monetary union for the EEC, but Thatcher was opposed because she saw the free market as more benign than fixed exchange rates, and was also concerned about further European integration. Nevertheless, threats to resign by Howe and Nigel Lawson, the Chancellor of the Exchequer, led Thatcher, at a European summit at Madrid in June 1989, to promise to join the ERM.

In July 1989, Howe was removed from the Foreign Office and made Deputy Prime Minister, but without being given power, which left him very bitter. That October, Lawson resigned in large part because of disagreement with Thatcher over his support for shadowing the Deutschmark, which was an indirect form of membership of the ERM and therefore unwelcome to Thatcher. He had supported shadowing the Deutschmark in order to deal with fiscal indiscipline. Feeling weakened, Thatcher was reluctantly prevailed on to join the ERM on 5 October 1990, in part by John Major, the new Chancellor of the Exchequer, and by Hurd, the new Foreign Secretary. Each of them seriously failed to appreciate the possible political and economic costs. Labour fully supported the policy.

Thatcher, however, made it very obvious that she had no intention of accepting further integration within the EEC, not least a single currency. She correctly saw that monetary union was designed to lead to political union. That path was clearly laid out by the meeting of EEC leaders in the European Council in Rome that October 1990, which declared, 'The European Community will have a single currency which will be an expression of its unity and identity.' Thatcher firmly rejected this conclusion, and Britain was the sole state to vote against further economic and monetary union, touching off the immediate crisis that led to her fall.

Having resigned on 1 November 1990, in anger at Thatcher's clear-cut, indeed strident opposition to further integration, Howe attacked Thatcher in a speech in the Commons on 13 November for being unable to accept debate and for her policy on Europe. He claimed that this policy was leading to Britain becoming isolated and ineffective. Howe also encouraged a leadership bid by Michael Heseltine, another supporter of the EEC, who had left the Cabinet in 1986 over the Westland affair, in which he had clashed with Thatcher over whether the Westland helicopter manufacturer should be taken over by an American company (as she wished) or by a European consortium, the goal he unsuccessfully sought. Having done insufficiently well against Heseltine on the first ballot, Thatcher, after initially resolving to fight on, stood down from the second ballot and resigned in order to ensure Heseltine's defeat.

An instructive contrast in political cultures, one arising also from the takeover of assets and from European integration, was provided by the promise given Mitterrand by Kohl that, as part of French acceptance of German unification, French companies would be allowed to acquire East German state-owned companies in the rapid privatisation that was pushed through. This served to limit German governmental commitments in the local economy. Elf

Aquitaine, an oil giant with close links to the French state, bought an oil refinery and, in return, paid about 256 million francs to various lobbyists, including 'provisions' for Kohl and other Christian Democratic politicians. The eventual funding scandal led to Kohl, after retirement in 1998, being stripped of his title of honorary chairman of the CDU.

1990–7

Major, who succeeded Thatcher as Prime Minister in November 1990, sought to distance himself from her confrontational style, and had initially spoken about his desire to place Britain 'at the heart of Europe'. In the strongly contested election to the Conservative European Committee, Bill Cash, a prominent Eurosceptic MP, was voted out in favour of Norman Fowler, and pro-Europeans won every office. *The Best Future for Britain*, the Conservative election manifesto for the 1992 general election, somewhat wistfully declared: 'Britain is at the heart of Europe; a strong and respected partner. We have played a decisive part in the development of the Community over the past decade.' This, however, was a statement of aspiration, not reality, one that linked the global role that British Conservatives largely sought, and moreover demonstrated in the 1991 Gulf War, with a European one that most believed necessary but without significant enthusiasm. Britain was certainly not at the heart of Europe, and particularly not of the Europe of the EEC.

Thatcher's fall was not to settle the political and fiscal relationship between Britain and its European partners, which was increasingly problematic, creating growing difficulties for the cohesion of the Conservative Party. Seeking to defend national interests, Major resisted the concentration of decision-making within the EEC at the level of supranational institutions. At the Maastricht conference of European leaders held in December

1991, Major obtained an opt-out clause from stage three of economic and monetary union, the single currency, and from the 'Social Chapter', which was held likely to increase social welfare and employment costs, to threaten the competitiveness and autonomy of British industry, and therefore not to be in Britain's competitive interest. Major also ensured that the word 'federal' was excluded from the Maastricht Treaty, although that was more a victory of style than substance.

Nevertheless, the greater integration agreed at Maastricht was too much for the Eurosceptics in the Conservative Party. The Treaty on European Union, signed at Maastricht on 7 February 1992, created the European Union (EU), the new term an indication of the new prospectus. Every citizen of an EEC member state was to be a citizen of this Union, with certain rights in every EEC country. The treaty also extended the scope and powers of the EEC (renamed the European Community, or EC) over its members, and announced that 'a common foreign and security policy is hereby established'. The scope of the Commission, the EEC's executive branch, was expanded over more areas of policy, including transport, education and social policy, the last a dangerously vague concept that threatened a progressive expansion of competence. In pursuit of 'a high degree of convergence of economic performance', member states were required to accept the fiscal discipline demanded by the Commission and the Council of Ministers. In addition, the ability of national ministers to exercise a veto on the Council of Ministers on behalf of national interests was restricted, while the powers of the European Parliament over legislation were extended. There were clear aspects of federalism in the division of powers between the EC and individual states.

The role of the Eurosceptics within the Conservative Party was increased because the election held on 9 April 1992 left Major with only a small parliamentary majority (of 21), which made it difficult for him to follow a policy on 'Europe' that was not at risk from wrecking opposition. This was a situation that Theresa May was to face with a vengeance after the 2017 election totally failed to provide her with the larger majority she had sought in order to push through Brexit against critics within, as well as beyond, the Conservative Party.

In the 1990s, Euroscepticism also provided a means for disaffected Thatcherites, angry at Thatcher's fall, to express their fury, and ensured that the issue became a key one in steadily more bitter dividedness. The struggle to win parliamentary endorsement for Maastricht, in the shape of the European Communities (Amendment) Bill, badly weakened the government, which had to make its passage a vote of confidence. In what Major referred to as 'gruesome trench warfare', the Conservative vote against the treaty eventually encompassed one-fifth of the party's backbench MPs. The Paving Motion designed to take the Maastricht Bill through passed on 4 November 1992, but the vote was 319 to 316, a majority of only three. The treaty only became law on 20 July 1993.[26] A year later, as a separate process, the Channel Tunnel was opened.

The crisis led to the establishment of right-wing political groups that helped lead to the focusing of interests on the European issue. The United Kingdom Independence Party (UKIP) was founded in 1992 as a sequel to the Anti-Federalist League, and the European Foundation followed in 1993. This was not simply a development on the national level, for in 1992 the European Anti-Maastricht Alliance was established. However, European-level opposition to further integration proved difficult to arrange or apply.

Denmark, France and Ireland all held referenda on the treaty, referenda the Commission was happy to ignore, but, aware of the unpopularity of its policy (and more generally of the government), the Major cabinet refused to do so. This refusal lacked a constitutional basis as there had already been a referendum in 1975. It was also unpopular, ignoring a Maastricht Referendum Campaign that collected over half a million signatures for its petition to Parliament. The failure to hold a referendum provided James Goldsmith, a multi-millionaire financier without any background in parliamentary politics, with an issue for mobilising discontent by means of a Referendum Party, and also helped weaken the base of the Conservative government, not least by dispiriting activists, which contributed to failure in the subsequent 1997 election. The government's 'wait and see' line over British participation in the single currency encouraged doubt and was not a way to rally support.

The government's reputation for economic management had already been crippled by another aspect of European policy. On 'Black Wednesday', 16 September 1992, an over-valued exchange rate, the interest-rate policies of the Bundesbank, and speculators forced sterling out of the European Exchange Rate Mechanism (ERM). Major had supported entry at what was an over-valued exchange rate because he believed that this would squeeze inflation out of the British economy and thus create an environment for growth. The government, however, found itself forced to respond to the financial policies of the strongest economy in the ERM, Germany, and unable to persuade the Bundesbank to reduce its interest rates. The Bundesbank put the control of German inflation, seriously threatened as a consequence of the budget deficit arising from German unification in 1990, above the prospects for British growth, and thus reminded ministers of the disadvantages of close international ties. The French government had similarly hoped that competition once France joined the ERM would squeeze inflation out of the economy, but, not least with closer ties with Germany, it was in a better political position to influence the resulting situation. Britain had joined the ERM in October 1990 at the rate of 2.95 Deutschmark to the pound, and this obliged the government to raise interest rates to defend the pound when its value reached the bottom of the permitted exchange-rate band at 2.82 Deutschmark. This helped lead to an economic depression and an unsustainable deficit, but the Major government felt that it had to stay in for political reasons.

Departure from the ERM in 1992 was a humiliating defeat for fiscal policy, and one that involved the Bank of England, in a futile effort to stay in, deploying over £15 billion from its reserves while interest rates were raised to 15 per cent. In practice, however, the exit brought crucial benefits, enabling Britain, in fiscal independence from the EU, to manage its own finances and to become a leading offshore financial centre, and helping encourage economic growth from the mid-1990s. In the 1990s, British GDP rose by an annual average of 2.3 per cent, which compared favourably with the leading ERM economies: 1.9 per cent for France and 1.3 per cent for Germany. In a major article in the *European* of 8 October 1992, Thatcher wrote:

> This Conservative government, like its predecessors, should have as its main priority the maintenance of our constitutional freedoms, our democratic institutions, and the accountability of Parliament to the people ... Thanks to the decision to float the pound, we now have a chance to follow an economic policy that puts British needs first ... We are warned, from home and abroad, that it would be a national humiliation if Britain were left in the 'slow lane' while others sped towards economic and monetary union. But ... a 'two-tier' Europe would at least enable the different groups of Europe to pursue different visions.

At the time, however, the crisis created an abiding impression of inept Conservative leadership, one that was to contribute to the election defeat in 1997. Major and his Chancellor of the Exchequer, Norman Lamont, had both staked the credibility of the government's entire economic and counter-inflationary strategy on membership of the ERM shortly before Britain was humiliatingly forced out of it. It was not that the electorate understood the ERM or the implications for British policy of coming out of it, but what they did know from the media was that it was a massive failure of Conservative policy upon which the party had staked its credibility. The result was seen in an immediate catastrophic collapse in Conservative electoral support based largely on its irrevocable loss of a substantial lead over Labour in terms of perceived economic competence. Despite a significant recovery in economic performance by 1996–7, there was to be no 'feel-good factor'. The Labour Party was able to divert attention from the extent to which, under the leadership of John Smith in 1992–4, it had backed the ERM and EMU.

In a television address on 29 March 1993, Mitterrand declared, 'Without a common monetary system, there is no Europe.' The ERM was the prelude to the European currency, the euro. Being outside the ERM permitted Britain not only independent economic management, but also an attitude of 'wait and see' over the currency. Unacceptable to the Eurosceptics, who wanted a commitment not to enter the currency, this attitude at least ensured a reduction of tension over Europe in the last stage of the Major government. Nevertheless, this was only in relative terms, and the background had been a grim one.

The continued Eurosceptic revolt against the leadership forced the whips to treat votes on Europe as if they were votes of confidence, with the implicit threat of destroying the government. Despite this moral pressure, the Eurosceptic wing of the party harassed its frontbench up to the end of the parliamentary session just before the 1997 election. In November 1994, a Bill enabling an increase in the budget contribution to the EU that was opposed by Eurosceptics was made a matter of confidence by the cabinet. This led to eight MPs losing the whip,[27] which cost the government its overall majority, although the whip was restored in April 1995. Eurosceptics, however, played a key role in supporting John Redwood's unsuccessful challenge for the leadership later that year.

From the other side of the Party, Heseltine, who then became Deputy Prime Minister, and Kenneth Clarke, the Chancellor of the Exchequer, took a more 'pro-European' line, reducing Major's room for manoeuvre considerably, but without winning the government any popularity or giving it any impetus. Instead, their policies helped win support for the disruptive challenge mounted by the Referendum Party. These problems were exploited by Labour and, indeed, helped encourage it in feeling that being pro-European was a way not only to define distance from the Conservatives, but also to do so in a way that would appear progressive. There was much about 1995–7 that is politically relevant today.

In 1996, problems came from another direction when concern about BSE (bovine spongiform encephalopathy or 'mad cow disease') in Britain led to a ban on the export of British beef by the EU. The unwillingness of the EU to accept British assurances once the beef herd had been cleared, and a reasonable suspicion that this was motivated by self-interest, particularly on the part of France, greatly affected public debate in Britain. The iconic significance of beef in terms of centuries of British self-identification was brought out by contemporary commentators. The long-term impact of these events is difficult to assess, but they presumably increased the sense of an abandonment of national identity as well as the national interest. The crisis also led to a serious clash between the EU and the government, with Britain taking the symbolically potent step of not appearing at meetings of the Council of Ministers: the 'empty chair policy' that had been employed by the French in the early 1960s.

By weakening the Conservatives in the 1997 election, the Referendum Party helped Labour,[28] although the government's record over the ERM, its broken promises over taxation, and the complete collapse of electoral faith in its economic and governing competence, compounded by the manifest divisions within its ranks, had made a Labour victory inevitable. The Referendum Party won no seats, but indicated the growing division on the right, a division in which foreign policy, in the sense of Europe, played the central role. The post-Thatcher Conservative Party had been swallowed up in the European issue in the 1990s, and the issue remained divisive and electorally significant thereafter. It helped ensure that Clarke did not become party leader. The division is the background to the inability to settle on policy in 2018 and to the bitterness linked to the issue.

1997–2010

In part, the electoral significance of 'Europe' eventually came to relate to the challenge from UKIP, a challenge that became more potent in the 2010s, only to collapse totally due to divisions and failure in 2017–18. Indeed, although deriving strength from disaffected voters across the political spectrum, UKIP under Nigel Farage essentially sought to reposition the right and to offer a different current of conservatism from that presented by the Conservative Party. This approach encompassed foreign policy principally in terms of a defining hostility to the EU. There was a difference between 'scepticism' and outright hostility, although the latter drew on the former.

As a consequence, the Conservative Party, in opposition from 1997 to 2010, as the leading part of a coalition government in 2010–15, and as a governing party in 2015–17, increasingly had to consider and present its position in response not only to its own divisions, the Labour opposition and ongoing events, but also with reference to a rival conservative party. Although there was no direct or indirect linkage, UKIP was another iteration of the 'ultras' of the past, even if Farage denied that the party stood for '1950s Britain, albeit with the stocks back on the green'.[29] Many of the tensions were familiar to those mindful of historical episodes, for example the rivalries between Hanoverian Tories and Jacobites, and the tensions in the 1790s and the nineteenth century.

The historical range of reference in the debate over 'Europe' could be surprising. Thus, in 2005 Cash, a Conservative MP and chairman of the European Foundation, a Eurosceptic movement, referred to the European Union Treaty:

> The Treaty was a prerogative act by the Government today no less significant in its denial of our democracy and the role of our voters in General Elections to choose their laws and their government than at any time it has evolved since the time of the Stuarts when Charles II signed the Secret Treaty of Dover in 1670 with France. The object was to bypass the English Parliament in a deal with Louis XIV of France in return for his political and financial support so long as Charles did not recall Parliament. Eventually all this led to the throwing out of Charles's successor, James II, the Glorious Revolution, the Bill of Rights, the assertion of Parliamentary rule and the evolution of our present-day democratic system of government. This is not historical pedantry. This is about what the people of this country have fought and died for for centuries.[30]

Nevertheless, Cash's stance enjoyed only very limited national political traction in the early 2000s. Support within the Conservative parliamentary party was far from intense, although the party leader, Michael Howard, was pledged to EU renegotiation, that is the repatriation of power, while in 2005 the Conservatives voted against the second reading of the European Union Bill. However, the Conservatives were in a minority and there was scant sign that Britain would significantly change its relationship with the EU.

Cultural Continuities and Discontinuities

The cultural continuity that had lasted from the Victorian period had been destroyed, largely in the 1960s, although with major changes earlier and later. Not only the intellectual élite but also, to a degree, the political leadership of the parties withdrew from engagement with the needs and concerns of most of the population. The long tradition of British history that had prevailed from the Revolution Settlement after the Glorious Revolution of 1688–9 largely collapsed. The empire disappeared, as did Britain's role as a leading maritime nation, and some leading Conservatives, notably Cameron, came to criticise, and apologise for, the imperial legacy. It became apparent that British history had, in large part, meant British Empire history, much of which had now passed. In contrast, the 'little Britishness' characteristic of the post-war period is more recently and insecurely grounded. Indeed, part of the working-class support that the Conservatives attracted in Scotland may have been connected with that party's support for the empire, and, as the empire disappeared, so did such support. At the same time, support was also derived from the sectarian divide between Irish Catholics and Scottish Protestants, which sustained working-class conservatism in the West of Scotland, just as it did in Lancashire into the 1950s and 1960s.

The cultural and religious continuity of the country was greatly compromised in the 1960s, notably with an accentuation of the longer-term decline in the position, popularity and relevance of the established churches and with the ascendancy of secular values. In addition, Americanism and globalisation weakened native styles, whether in food or in diction, with all that they meant for distinctiveness and continuity. The political culture was also changed, as traditional expressions of freedom, liberty, and respect for both law and individual rights were altered by governmental and institutional priorities and interests. These changes did not begin in the 1960s, but they gathered pace then. There had already been a major change in tone in the 1950s.

Not only the historical references that were usable changed but also, more significantly, the frame of reference. National exceptionalism and national destiny, both ideas particularly important to the Eurosceptics and their sense of necessary distance from the Continent, were under pressure, not least as providential concepts of history were totally discarded. The changing historical frame of reference was particularly true of the loss of empire. The 250th anniversary in 2009 of James Wolfe's victory outside Québec was largely ignored, as, for example, were the anniversaries in 2013 of the Peace of Utrecht (1713) and the Peace of Paris (1763).

In many respects, this loss of empire represented an important discontinuity. However, younger generations did not feel this, and, for many of the young in particular, the military aspects of Thatcher's funeral in 2013, for example, appeared part of a past age. This dissociation is particularly apparent because the historical memory and imagination of specific generations in time replace what has gone before. As a consequence, the 'deep history' that was resonant for Churchill and his generation is no longer present. Moreover, membership in the EU put pressures on traditional assumptions about national identity and interests. This influenced both Britain's relationships within Europe and the debate about them.

6

BRITAIN AND EUROPE TODAY

'Who then will be the next Prime Minister?' (January 2016). The world certainly changes. I asked this question of a friend, and Conservative MP, who told me it would be Boris Johnson or George Osborne and that the issue would be how to stop Johnson. Enquiring whether Theresa May might be the next Prime Minister, I was told that she was too unpopular among her fellow Conservative MPs to make the final shortlist of two candidates. Well, two and a half years later, May is Prime Minister, Osborne is a newspaper editor, Johnson is a back-bencher, and my friend has lost his seat.

Writing about the present is always difficult, and more so in a book than a newspaper or a magazine, as the period from writing to publication is longer. The current British–European crisis has both short-term and long-term causes. The range of factors, attitudes, views and rhetorical tropes is such that the question of typicality is a vexed one, as is the attempt to dissect lines of influence. It can be difficult to distinguish between goals and methods, not least as the international and domestic costs of the latter can compromise the former. Policy, furthermore, needs to be separated from rhetoric. There is also the problem that policy choices and, even more, assumptions are set on a continuum, rather than being clearly differentiated.

The serious fiscal and political crisis in the Eurozone of the early 2010s encouraged those within the EU, notably in the Commission, who wanted greater convergence, and, in response, it led to a wider process of Conservative criticism of the EU. In 2011, the European Union Act proposed a referendum if further powers were transferred to the European institution. There was also increasing discussion among Conservative MPs about the repatriation of powers 'from Brussels' and, indeed, of withdrawal from the EU as an option. This discussion became more prominent from 2013.

So also did an initially largely separate anxiety about national identity expressed in unease about large-scale immigration as well as, more specifically, concerns about aspects of EU policy, from the lapse of the transitional controls on migration from new members, to EU policies for the allocation of immigrants among member states. The significance of the free movement of labour within the EU clashed with anxieties about national identity and a range of issues.

The concerns expressed by Cameron[1] and others proved an instructive contrast with the Conservative manifesto for the 2009 European election, which stated: 'Our MEPs will support the further enlargement of the EU, including to Ukraine, Belarus, Turkey, Georgia and the countries of the Balkans, if they wish to achieve EU membership, however distant that prospect may be in some cases.' In December 2013, Cameron said at the close of the EU summit that he would use Britain's veto to block the accession of any new countries, such as Serbia and Albania, unless rules were changed to prevent 'mass population movements across Europe'. Nick Clegg, the Liberal Democrat Deputy Prime Minister in the coalition government, claimed that the issue was 'the biggest dividing line in politics today'.[2]

In June 2012, John Baron, a Conservative backbench MP, delivered a letter from a hundred colleagues demanding a referendum on the EU. The challenge from the United Kingdom Independence Party (UKIP) and disaffected Conservatives caused Cameron, in accordance with a promise made in January 2013 (under pressure from colleagues), to go into the 2015 general election undertaking to renegotiate the terms of British membership in the EU, and then to put continued membership to a referendum. He appears to have anticipated a continuation of the coalition with the Liberal Democrats, and having therefore (willingly) to abandon the promise as the price of a renewed coalition, as the Liberal Democrats were against any such referendum. Indeed, pressure from within the Conservative Party over the referendum was in part a matter of push-back against the coalition. In 2010, this had brought Cameron control over both Parliament and his parliamentary party, but without satisfying a significant tranche of the latter, notably on the right. Instead of a continuation of the coalition, in 2015 Cameron unexpectedly won an overall majority, in large part at the expense of the Liberal Democrats.

An additional, maybe alternative, explanation suggests that Cameron, from 2013, was in general concerned about the UKIP challenge and sought to staunch Tory defections to it by means of the promise. Two MPs had defected to UKIP in August–September 2014 (going on to retain their seats, Clacton and Maidstone, in by-elections), giving it a parliamentary presence, and more defections were rumoured or threatened. If so, this was a classic instance of a tactical solution that created a strategic problem, one that reflected the extent to which politics are lived in the present. Whatever the result, it was clear that Cameron would be judged as someone who had taken a great risk, as indeed had been the case with the earlier referenda on proportional representation (2011) and on Scottish independence (2014), both of which were rejected when it came to the vote.

Having won the election, Cameron was unable to secure many concessions on the terms of British membership in the EU, and certainly not those he had suggested he would obtain and that he had pursued in exhaustive negotiations. Cameron won agreement to restrictions on benefits for new arrivals for up to seven years, concessions to the City of London, and an opt-out from 'ever closer union', but these did not amount to what much of the public wanted and many expected.

More seriously, despite his strong efforts, an impression of defeat, indeed of total defeat, was created. This rejection of Cameron, while understandable, represented a major failure of perception and policy by both the European Commission and the leading member states. In some respects, there was a parallel to Germany's refusal to help Britain (unlike France) at the time of the 1992 ERM crisis. It appears to have been expected that the referendum would be won by Cameron, that the episode would be yet another in which the British had to yield, and that, as a consequence, it could serve to strengthen federalist tendencies.

Instead, Cameron found himself in an exposed position during the referendum debate, obliged to defend British membership in the face of considerable public reluctance on the issue and of a Conservative Party that was totally and very publicly divided. In place of positive arguments for continued membership, the general theme from the Remain side was that of the financial, economic and political dangers of being outside the EU. A dire picture of national isolation was painted, notably by George Osborne, the Chancellor of the Exchequer, supported by a visit by President Obama, in what critics referred to, fairly or unfairly but certainly memorably, as 'project fear'. This picture reflected a sense that the United States could not be relied on to support Britain's interests, and also an awareness of a new set of international challenges different from those of the Cold War but, nevertheless, still serious.

The difficult economic and fiscal situation of the country proved a key context, as it had done throughout the post-war period. Indeed, the 2016 referendum brought to the fore and focused many of the tensions and issues of contemporary British history. These included immigration and the British question. Popular worries about immigration played a potent role in the debate. The immigration issue was not in fact one solely about the EU, as many immigrants came from non-EU countries, notably in Africa and South Asia. Moreover, much of the public discussion was ill-informed, not least failing adequately to appreciate the value of immigrants or to address the ethical issues involved.

Conversely, the sense of a disproportionate rate of change was captured by, and for, a public some of whom claimed to be 'overwhelmed'. Brexit campaigners predicted that continued membership would lead to an annual immigration of 300,000 people and would rapidly result in a UK population of 80 million, and drew attention to what they claimed was the risk that Turkey would join the EU. Cameron correctly argued that there was no current prospect of long-standing accession negotiations with Turkey leading to such an outcome, but the immigration question, notably over Turkey, touched all sorts of subliminal issues. That Turkey represented apparent Islamicisation made it a far more potent issue, and notably so due to the immigration into the EU from Syria and North Africa at that juncture. This was very much a case of contingencies to the fore.

Less contentiously, given high unemployment rates in much of the EU and attractive minimum wage provisions in Britain, continued inward movement at a high rate appeared likely. Indeed, migration to Britain had helped serve as a safety-valve on the Continent during the recession over the previous eight years. This immigration had not caused unemployment in Britain but it probably kept wage rates lower than they would otherwise have been.

The eventual referendum result surprised most commentators, even though the polls had shown a move to leave the EU a fortnight prior to the vote. In practice, a very similar move happened in the Scottish referendum at around the same stage in 2014, and also in 1975 in the EU referendum, but without any eventual vote to leave. The polls on average in 2016 showed each side on percentage support in the low to mid-forties. These numbers did not, however, as anticipated, underestimate support for Remain. There was the difficulty for pollsters of reaching the people more likely to vote, who are the people with jobs, active lives and more affluence.

The history of referenda suggested that undecideds break 2 to 1 for the status quo whatever the question: but that did not happen in 2016. Studies, moreover, indicate that up to 30 per cent change their mind in referenda in the last few days and even on the day. These points interact with a key aspect of human psychology: humans are loss-averse and tend to favour the status quo on anything when it gets to the decision point. This helps explain why there are few one-term British governments. Studies also show that, as the vote nears and people actually have to exercise their vote, rather than expressing an off-the-cuff point of view, they have a frightened sense of responsibility, not just to themselves but to their friends, family and community. That interacts with the previous point to make them nervous and more conservative and therefore, it was thought by many, including the stock market and foreign exchange dealers, more likely to vote Remain. Fear about the economy, accordingly, it was widely anticipated, would probably trump undoubted anger and concern over immigration.

In the event, Brexit, with 17,410,742 votes cast, won the majority. On a high participation rate for the UK, 72 per cent of the electorate, just under 52 per cent overall, voted for Brexit, although London, Scotland and Northern Ireland voted very strongly for Remain, as did graduates and the young. In the North, strong support for Brexit from white working-class areas swayed the result. The vote for Brexit was 70 per cent in Hartlepool, 68.3 per cent in Barnsley, 62 per cent for South Tyneside, 61.3 per cent for Sunderland, and 57.5 per cent for Durham. More affluent cities supported Remain, notably Leeds and Newcastle, but the majorities were slight: Newcastle voted 50.4 per cent for Remain, producing the first warning sign for Cameron,[3] and Leeds 50.3 per cent. At the same time, Brexit did well across much of the South, apart from in London and university cities such as Exeter. England was divided, but less so geographically than it might appear or than subsequent response to the vote in the North suggested. Although the general perception is that working-class voters in the North of England were responsible for Brexit, a perception frequently accompanied with pejorative comments, the vote in the South was more important than that in the North owing to the large number of voters there.

In practice, on the national scale, a majority of homeowners who had no mortgage voted for Brexit, as, very differently, did social and council tenants. Only a majority of private renters and of people with mortgages voted for Remain. Polls suggested that 96 per cent of UKIP voters at the 2015 general election and 58 per cent of the Conservative voters voted Brexit, compared to 37 per cent for Labour, 36 per cent for the SNP, 30 per cent for the Liberal Democrats, and 25 per cent for the Greens. Although seen as right-wing by most, UKIP's economic policies were of the left.

Daniel Hannan, a Eurosceptic MEP, declared June 23 'Independence Day' while Nigel Farage of UKIP proclaimed a victory for 'ordinary people'. This was not the sole view. A French academic commentator, Pierre Manent, pointed out that 'the British political class had not given its soul to the European idea as had its French counterpart'.[4]

At a different level, the question of British cohesion came to the fore, as it was widely anticipated that a Brexit vote might increase pressure for another Scottish referendum on independence, despite the serious economic and fiscal problems created for Scotland by the fall in the price of oil. Whereas all the Scottish council areas voted for Remain, and 55.8 per cent of the Northern Irish who voted voted for Remain, 17 out of the 22 Welsh councils voted for Brexit. Brexit gained a majority in the industrial areas of South Wales, including 56.4 per cent for Merthyr Tydfil and 62 per cent for Blaenau Gwent. Wales was a major recipient of EU funding as was another Brexit area, Cornwall. Of the English vote 53.4 per cent was for Brexit, but only 38 per cent of the Scottish. On 22 July 2016, in the heated atmosphere after the referendum, a YouGov poll claimed that one in nine Londoners wanted independence, while a quarter favoured a London parliament with powers similar to the Scottish Assembly.

There were also questions about the fabric of national life. The murder in 2016 of Jo Cox, a Labour MP campaigning for Britain to remain in the EU, allegedly by a Brexit supporter who supposedly shouted 'Britain first, keep Britain independent', created anxiety about the vulnerability of British democracy. Significantly, the alleged assassin lived in a Yorkshire constituency with a high rate of unemployment, a constituency once known for the manufacture of textiles and cars, but with both having ended many years ago. From another angle, the rarity of such attacks since 1970, other than by IRA terrorists, was notable. The net effect served to underline the range of uncertainties that faced Britain.

Uncertainties related, and continue to relate, to the wider world. Unprecedented population growth, especially in Africa, provided a context for the debate over migration within Europe, notably as a result of greatly increased immigration in 2015, largely from Syria, Libya, Afghanistan, Iraq and Eritrea, and of contentious EU attempts to redistribute immigrants. In 2018, these factors helped in the establishment of populist governments in Austria, Italy and Slovenia, and in the re-election of one in Hungary. Separately, instability in the Middle East and Russian sabre-rattling threw attention on the EU's inability to work out effective defence and foreign policy arrangements. Grave fears over American leadership, notably under President Trump, accentuated this concern, but also encouraged pressure for such arrangements.

It was readily apparent that Britain had serious political, economic and social problems, irrespective of whether or not it was in the EU. In part, the EU debate was a significant distraction from these problems but, in part, it contributed directly to them. The strong and sustained opposition to the Brexit process displayed after the referendum, in many cases by people who had not bothered to vote or canvass prior to the referendum, contributed to uncertainty, as did the total failure of the Brexiteers to offer an adequate plan and certainly one that would stand up to the shock of reality, notably in terms of negotiations with the European Union. In part, continued opposition to the referendum result reflected the extent to which there was a genuine division of opinion over the issue, but there were also serious questions of consent and governability, including those over the future of the United Kingdom.

The increasingly bad-tempered debate repeatedly led to a failure to seek agreement, even though the essential point remains clear. Britain is a European country, but that does not dictate any particular political arrangement. Unfortunately, this proved unhelpful to polemicists and was therefore widely ignored. The emotional weight of the issue did not encourage measured restraint. Indeed, the virulence of some academic commentators proved particularly notable.

So many uncertainties in practice are to the fore. Each added speculation and hypotheses to current information. Uncertainties also served to challenge theoretical frameworks and to put into question historical perspectives. These uncertainties relate both to Britain and to the Continent, and it is never clear how to rank them and what causal links should be prioritised. To turn to Britain, it is unclear how far Brexit will undermine the Union and, more generally, reopen British questions, and, separately, how far it will liberalise the British economy. Such uncertainties were pushed back as the very process of implementing Brexit became not only what Brexit meant but also whether it would occur.

As far as the Continent is concerned, it is unclear whether President Macron will really be able to reverse the Socialist tide that France has been riding since 1981 and that has pushed down its trend rate of growth. It is unclear whether the euro will continue to give Germany an unassailable economic advantage. In 2018, Hungary, Italy and Poland all displayed a willingness to oppose either the EU or its major constituent powers, or both, the new Italian government being vociferous about both France and Germany. It is unclear whether Eurocrats reflect the views of the underlying governments, or whether they have seized power so that the EU is out of control.

Moreover, there are fundamental questions about the long-term stability and viability of the EU. A lack of linkage between populists, on the left and right, and, on the other hand, the drivers of the European 'project', as well as the matter of unfunded liabilities and a dysfunctional fiscal system, created questions about the ability of the EU to solve its problems. These questions were pertinent whether or not Britain was a member. It is unclear whether it is in the EU's interests to accommodate Britain or to be hostile, or which approach will prevail in the short, medium or long term.

Changing global power politics are also significant, notably deep strains between the United States and Europe including

Britain. It is unclear what an American-lite European security order might look like for Britain and the Continent. British security guarantees in theory provide a form of continuing commitment and leverage in the Continent, but that appears of limited consequence for the European Commission, and it is unclear how Britain can take advantage of these guarantees.

Strategic issues in part reflect the role of geopolitics. As an island power, Britain, like Japan with regard to China, not only had physical separation, but could also afford to be detached somewhat from the traditional geopolitical concerns that occupied the European land powers, notably France and Germany. Paranoid about German power, French foreign security policy found the EU a vehicle for a continued French role in the context of post-war imperial decline.

For Britain, there is a different security rationale from those of France and Germany, and a different cost-benefit analysis for continued membership. And so also into the future. Britain was semi-detached from the EU 'project' prior to the 2016 referendum and the latter has essentially changed the conditions of this semi-detachment. The challenge will be to use national structures effectively so as to maintain confidence in a democratic politics and culture.

Aside from the future of the EU, there was, and is, the case of the broader significance of the referendum for Britain's place in the world since 1945. This is unclear, but the referendum suggests that fundamental discontinuities can arise from particular circumstances at specific moments. How readily Britain will be able to maintain good relations with the EU, and to define a viable economic, political and strategic relationship with the remainder of the world, is uncertain and a matter of contention. We will live that future.

7

DEBATING THE LINKS

Applying the past to the present is inherently problematic and suffused with politics. Gazing ahead is especially dangerous. Developments in Eastern Europe and the former Soviet Union in the late 1980s and early 1990s underlined the unpredictable nature of change and thus raised question marks against claims about the nature and necessary course both of Europe and of relations between its parts. Such claims have been, and continue to be, exceptionally varied, and any summary, especially if in terms of British exceptionalism versus Britain as a necessary member of a united Europe, would be too simple. Arguably, that has also proved to be the case with the questions of what both Brexit and Remain mean.

Not least, there is the question 'Which Europe?' Although the EU can be regarded as a solution to this problem, certainly seeks to be so, and has expanded and is expanding to that end, this leaves not only a very ragged as well as questionable public history, but also a problematic present. The past can be readily addressed by pointing out not only the many historical contradictions within the Europe of the past, but also the questionable global implications of the process of definition. In particular, for much of the last six centuries, a large part of Eastern Europe was part of a very different cultural and political world, that of the Ottoman empire. An Islamic imperial state with its capital at Constantinople (Istanbul), this spent much of its history in conflict with Christian powers, and did so until its fall.

Modern scholars fruitfully search for parallels between Christian and Ottoman governments and societies. However, to contemporaries, the Ottomans were not so much non-European as anti-European. The Ottoman empire defined that which was not European, both tyranny and Islam, and presented both as a deadly threat to the alternative identity of Christendom.

Secondly, if 'Europe' did not enter into the Ottoman world, and certainly not fully so, it did successfully spread across the oceans. By 1750, as a result of both Ottoman conquests and overseas expansion, London, Paris and Madrid had more in common with colonial centres, such as Philadelphia, Québec and Havana, than they did with cities under Ottoman rule, such as Athens, Belgrade, Bucharest and Sofia. This situation remained the case over the following century. In addition, with a different geography, it was to resume during the Cold War, which very much divided Europe and provided the background for the establishment of what became the EU.

Relations between Western Europe and the trans-oceanic European world were transformed, from 1775, by successful moves for independence on the part of settler populations, first in what became the United States and then in Latin America. Nevertheless, their links with Western Europe remained strong. This was even more the case when, as with Australia, Canada and New Zealand, political and governmental relations between colonies and the imperial power were lessened peaceably and gradually. This history is questioned directly by the creation of a European history designed to go with the would-be modern identity, a history conceptually defended in terms of transnationalism.

Competition over history and histories has a its clear weight in the present. A notion of, indeed faith in, British exceptionalism has characterised much opposition to European integration, as with Hugh Gaitskell's 1962 claim (see ch. 5). Such claims could ignore or underplay the extent to which, repeatedly during its history, England had been a part of a trans-Channel polity. Indeed, close and important relations with Continental Europe have been a major theme of English, Scottish, Welsh, Irish and British history.

Yet that undoubted point implies neither uniformity nor, necessarily, a strong degree of European identity. Moreover, identity is neither exclusive nor a constant: a sense of collective self-awareness can include a number of levels or aspects of identification. These often develop, or are expressed, most clearly in hostility or opposition to other groups and their real or imagined aims and attributes; and these groups are frequently ones with which relations are close, at least in terms of living closely together. Indeed, the reality of overlapping senses of collective self-awareness can be very difficult, as can also be the processes of often continual adaptation to these senses.

Senses of identity are more amorphous, changeable and, at the same time, atavistic than the secular positivism implied by any stress on constitutions and laws might suggest. As such, they owe much to opposition, if not hostility, to other groups. For example, nineteenth-century German unification owed much to a sense of negative identity in which Germans distinguished themselves from the French, the Poles and the Austrians. This process helps explain nineteenth-century British ambivalence about Ireland.

For several decades, there has been a scholarly emphasis on the definition of a nation as 'an imagined political community'. As with much historical writing, to a considerable extent this is a matter of stating the obvious or, rather, of disguising it with a new vocabulary. It is readily apparent that, whereas England, Scotland, Wales and Ireland have longer and deeper identities, Britain as a political entity was in large part created by political actions and at specific moments, notably 1603 and 1707. Moreover, alongside a sharing of values, particularly empire and anti-Catholicism, among many but not all of the British, as well as a transfer of Englishness to the British stage and state, this creation owed something to the formulation and dissemination of new images. It is also clear that notions of nationhood were politically charged: that the ability to redefine patriotism, and to succeed in making a definition effective, could be of considerable importance in influencing domestic political developments. That continues to be part of the debate about British national identity and British relations with the Continent.

Changing notions of national interest could also affect external links. Thus, the First World War severed what had been very close relations with Germany, especially Protestant North Germany. The Communist revolution in Russia (1917) destroyed links with Russia that had been less close but were also important. Thereafter, the dominant British image of Europe was conditioned by the notion of a hostile Eastern Europe, one that threatened to engulf a freer or, at least, anti-Communist Western Europe, which thus became the bulwark of Britain rather than a threat to it.

Yet, ideas of dominant images have to be qualified by reference to the multiplicity of views: the political community is a product of more than one imagination, and the context within which views are expressed varies. Thus, whereas in the 2010s, with its democratic ethos and partially democratised political structure, British culture is generally understood to mean the culture of the people, in the nineteenth century and still earlier a more socially restricted notion of culture was regarded as pertinent. A social élite that had received a Classical education and that could read French had more in common with their Continental counterparts than with the bulk of the local population.

This situation, however, has been challenged as a consequence of social and cultural changes, most significantly those of the last half-century. Moreover, this challenge played a key role in the political crisis over Brexit. Populism became a term of abuse, on the pattern of past hostility to democratisation, notably nineteenth-century opposition to the expansion of the franchise.

As already argued, a stress on exceptionalism can derive in part from a reaction against a situation in which links with others are close. Furthermore, the theses of British exceptionalism and of Britain's close contacts with the Continent over the centuries are not incompatible, for the history of the European peoples and polities is one of considerable variety and complexity. This is a variety whose consequences can be readily grasped today not only in Britain, but also throughout Europe.

This issue related, and relates, directly to the question of what type of 'Europe' the EU will propose and offer in forthcoming years. Given the vitality of national political structures and cultures, the EU, arguably, will be most successful if it can accommodate the particular interests and views of nation states. Indeed, a policy based on superseding these states or making them redundant appears unrealistic, and in 2016, fairly or unfairly, this did appear to be the case to many of those who voted in the referendum and favoured sovereignty over economic considerations. Inherently, that position is difficult to trade off against those economic considerations, not least because each involves questions of prediction and risk that are inherently unfixed in their possible impact.

The EU has certainly failed to replace the nation states of Europe as a focus for popular identity and thus loyalty or potential loyalty. If this is a measure of its failure, it is also a cause of it, if failure is to be defined as an inability to proceed to federalism. The central political problem in any community is the eliciting of consent. This is not simply a question of defining acceptable policies and selecting leaders who will be judged competent, but also reflects the nature of identification between people and government, which is a question of history, symbolism, and a sense of place and purpose. These, in turn, combine to produce an ideology that is more potent than the more intellectual and abstract creeds usually designated by that term. This is arguably strong in Britain, because of its political and institutional continuity with its nineteenth-century past, which is unusual within Europe.

Such a view, however, has to be qualified by noting that it is not true of Ireland. The creation of the Irish Free State was a fundamental change. While in Northern Ireland the nationalist Catholic population is alienated from the mainland government, the same is also true, although to a lesser extent, of much of the Scottish population. Many have a nationalist consciousness and a sense of antipathy to London-based institutions even if they do not vote Scottish Nationalist. The symbolic potency of British nationhood is stronger in England than in Scotland, in that a sense of 'Englishness' does not generally clash with the implications of 'Britishness'.

Despite all the talk of the failure and redundancy of the nation state and its need for replacement by supranational bodies and 'Euro-regions', it is the nation state that is most effective at eliciting and securing consent. It is no accident that Euro-federalism is endorsed most strongly by peoples whose nation states are recent and weak (in the face of regional and other divisions), Belgium and Italy, while Britain and indeed Denmark, where the state cannot be described in these terms, are more sceptical about the process.

At the same time, analysts of the British state who detect, indeed sometimes welcome, signs of its weakness are most prone to argue the need for a different political framework. This thesis is most relevant to those who feel frustrated and thwarted by the British state, most obviously nationalist movements in Scotland, Wales and Northern Ireland. Within England, there is also the question of opposition to the government of the day.

It is also possible to exaggerate the effectiveness of the nation state as a representative political unit. There is a kind of circularity: the nation state represents national interests effectively because its very existence defines those interests. What is less clear is that the interests thus defined, and pursued, by the nation state are the primary interests of the people of that state. Nevertheless, given that these interests do not exist clearly, except in the most basic terms, outside the political process, the nation state plays a crucial role in the discussion, definition and validation of such interests. Irrespective of a commitment to Europeanness, it is far from clear that a European political community can successfully fulfil the same function, and certainly so in terms of obtaining popular support, including in Britain.

This situation owes much to the role of historical formation in giving identities and meaning to the lives of political communities (in this case the British nation and also the English, Scottish and Welsh ones). Britishness is of course historically specific and is generally seen as having been formed after the Anglo-Scottish union of 1707. It could also be argued, however, that Britishness in the nineteenth century, and possibly until 1945, was quintessentially imperial. Thus, the 'Little Britishness' characteristic of the post-war period, and of Thatcherism in particular, is of very recent origin, maybe not as deeply rooted as is generally implied, and therefore possibly much more permeable (or vulnerable, depending on perspective) to Continental ideas and cultural idioms.

The situation is naturally more complex and nuanced than any either/or approach. In particular, it is crucially important to neglect neither contingencies, in the shape of the events and pressures of domestic and international developments, nor continuities, most obviously in terms of institutional, constitutional and political longevities.

As the nature and future development of the EU are matters of current controversy, it is not clear what precisely Britain might be expected to converge with or diverge from, remain with or leave, in the future. Furthermore, it is far from clear what the relationship between the EU and Europe will be, and it is therefore apparent that the question of Anglo-European relations should not be treated as, indeed reduced to, simply one of the relationship between Britain and the EU. Despite the major growth of the EU from 1972–3, a part of what is generally understood to be Europe, Switzerland and Norway, is not part of the EU, and this is likely to remain the case. Indeed, the Norway solution was one mentioned in 2018 as a possibility for Britain. Economic and religious links with Norway, moreover, have been closer than with much of Mediterranean Europe.

In some respects, the domination of Eastern Europe by a hostile Soviet Union until 1989 helped British and other politicians to avoid the question of defining the 'Europe' to which Britain and other states were committed. Political changes in that region, and the determination of the newly non-Communist states to join the EU, however, obliged politicians to address the issue. Nevertheless, the successive Yugoslav crises of the 1990s underlined the extent to which much of the British population did not feel directly engaged in Eastern European questions. So also, for example, with the more recent quarrel over the identity of Macedonia. The Continent of course has come ever closer, for example in terms of visual imagery, so that, thanks successively to photography, film and frequent cheap flights, the British public now sees the Continent and its peoples as never before. However, the mental cartography that defines Europe for most of the British population is one that offers at best a patchy picture away from Western Europe.

Europe itself can be variously defined, and this is the case both for the British and for others. It can be treated geographically, though once more precision is sought than the statement that it is located between Asia and the Atlantic, such a treatment is itself open to debate and dissension. Asia, moreover, is generally treated as starting with the Urals, which puts much of Russia, as well as all of Ukraine, in Europe. Indeed, the relationship between Russia and any definition of Europe is a matter of difficulty if logic (rather than politics) is to be pursued.

Europe can also be treated as a value system, a goal or an ideology, though such arguments create even more problems. Geographically, they can lead to Georgia and Armenia being placed in Europe. Arguments about a value system can take on more distinct form in the claim that Britain would be better off emulating the 'social market' economies of Western Europe, which have very much influenced the character and goals of the EU.

The attempt to treat Europe as an economic or administrative aggregation has greater point, as there is a legal entity, in the shape of the EU, that can be focused on, but it is clear that part of Europe will not be comprised in the EU. Moreover, criticism of its institutions will remain strong, and deservedly so, as in many respects they are scarcely fit for purpose, either politically or governmentally.

It is also highly questionable to adopt a view of Europe in which the quintessential definition of Europeanness is membership of the EU, and everything else is a falling away, a failure to realise potential which may, however, be recovered by good conduct and if a given public myth is adopted. Instead, the EU and Europe are not the same thing, and this would be the case even were they to be coterminous. They are different categories of identity.

Indeed, although some who were first opponents of the Maastricht treaty and subsequently supporters of Brexit may be self-confessed 'Little Englanders', others can quite legitimately claim that they are in no way 'anti-European', but simply want to see 'Europe' developing along different lines from the ones envisaged by Delors and the 'Euro-federalists'. This was certainly Thatcher's position, and, in addition, she prided herself on the role that Western firmness had played in the freeing of Eastern Europe from Soviet hegemony and Communism; her vision of Europe was far from restricted to the EU. Nevertheless, the identification of Europe with the EU has had much impact: British politicians talked in the 1960s and 1970s of 'entering Europe', and, in the 1980s, Thatcher's views on the EU led to her being presented as 'anti-European'. At the same time, there are pro-Europeans who are critical of the EU, and some of them support Brexit. In Britain, for example, this is the position of Michael Gove.

A public myth of European identity plays a major role as Europe is now conceived. Here another aspect of British divergence can be noted, for, while Britain bought membership, it did not buy the myth, a point clearly seen in the 2016 referendum when there was little public defence of the European myth, as opposed to prudential defences of membership. Indeed, if scepticism about the value of belonging to the EU and about its institutions is widespread, this is but a pale echo of the indifference or hostility that greets the European myth. The modern British may not be a flag-waving nation; most certainly they do not tend to wave the flag of Europe. British soldiers might go to kill, and be killed, in the Falklands in 1982 or Iraq and Afghanistan in the 2000s and 2010s, but there was scant enthusiasm for doing so for Europe, as was demonstrated in the 1990s when discussing any intervention other than humanitarian in Yugoslavia. At the same time, large-scale popular opposition in 2003 to forthcoming participation in the Iraq War was ignored.

Separately, Britain's departure from the Exchange Rate Mechanism on 16 September 1992, and the clear governmental reluctance to rejoin it, were popular with many. Already prior to that, the Major government had adopted 'subsidiarity' as the key phrase to describe an organisational, indeed constitutional, principle that would leave as much power and responsibility as possible with existing structures rather than with European institutions. This is a key subtext, whether or not Britain remains in the EU. The Prime Minister who won the second largest vote in a general election was May in 2017; the largest was Major in 1992. These facts, however, are a matter of widespread surprise. Blair, Thatcher and Cameron tend to be the chosen answers.

The European myth entailed, and continues to entail, anachronism, teleology and reification. In short, it is an echo of the national myths that have played such a major role in the creation of nation states. These myths, however, were grounded in the experience of particular political communities or nations; have over much of Europe had centuries to work (although in other areas far less time); can look back on a history of military and political challenges that have been surmounted; and are lent force by the institutions of states that reach into every community and life, for example through education. In contrast, none of these circumstances is true of the European myth.

There is a considerable historiography devoted to the concept of Europe. It is clear that for the post-Roman period until the French Revolution began in 1789 the nearest equivalent term was Christendom, and that this cannot be seen as a proto-Europe, however much the present myth of Europe requires such an anachronism. For Christendom, belief, not place, counted, and this produced a common ideology that was more potent than anything modern Europe possesses, as well as, in the form of the medieval Papacy, a distinctive form of government. Eastern Christendom, however, was not under the Papacy, and extended beyond modern conceptions of Europe into the Middle East and north-east Africa. That perspective tends to be overlooked by Western European Christians who focus their historical account of Europe on the Papacy.

Western Christendom was fragmented and greatly altered during that artificial construct the 'early modern period'—the sixteenth and seventeenth centuries—thanks to the Reformation, the development of state mechanisms and ideologies, the rise of vernacular languages, and the creation of extra-European empires. These changes did not contribute to a concept of Europe that meant much as far as its peoples and governments were concerned. The Revolutionary–Napoleonic period, on the other hand, witnessed not only a political struggle that absorbed the whole of the Continent, but also the formulation of universalist revolutionary and counter-revolutionary ideologies. The language of politics changed radically and the basic configuration of domestic political struggles was established for the nineteenth century.

The universalist and somewhat utopian language of the Revolutionary period might seem to lend itself to modern searchers for an alternative ideology to the nation state. However, it was associated with social division, political violence and French self-interest; hardly a better basis than the self-righteousness, shallowness and social condescension of so much of what has been termed the Enlightenment of the eighteenth century. Given the role of the Enlightenment, itself a reification, in the public myth of the EU, it is worth noting that the attitude of many of its intellectuals to the common people was harsh. The people were generally presented as ignorant, their beliefs the very antithesis of those of the enlightened. The peasantry were to be improved in spite of themselves. The language used to describe them was that used to discuss children or animals. The intellectuals dismissed what they disliked as superstitious, exaggerated the possibilities of change through education, and neglected the difficulties of turning aspirations into policies, the problems of government, the vitality of popular religiosity, and the disinclination of people to subordinate self-interest and their own notions of a just society to the views and self-righteousness of others. This neglect helped to produce frustration and confusion among some 'progressive' thinkers during the early years of the French Revolution, and to engender an attitude in which the creation and defence of a just society through terror appeared necessary.

It would clearly be ridiculous to imply that the modern European movement is moving in the same direction. In place of the national-cum-ideological hegemony sought by the French revolutionaries and, very differently, by Hitler, and the national dominance pursued by Napoleon and, again differently, Wilhelm II, there has been a resolute attempt with the EU to create a supranational system that seeks both to supersede national interests and to create a structure of national and institutional power-sharing. All the members of the EU are democracies, and the institutions of the EU are thus filled, directly or indirectly, as a consequence of democratic processes. The meaning of democracy can be very varied, and certainly is so within Europe, and there is an undoubted 'democratic deficit' within the EU, but democracy acts as a key constraint in its ideology and structure, one expressed in a variety of legal obligations.

Focusing on the difficulties confronting the attempt to create a plausible European public myth helps to explain some of the problems facing those that seek to displace the nation state from its position in popular loyalties. Moreover, the aggregate significance of the issue has increased with the rise in the number of member states. Shelving that level of identity is implausible for many that have joined since 2000, including Hungary and Poland.

Related but also separate, a sense of place and continuity is crucial to the harmony of individuals and societies. It is challenged by the continual process of change, a process that entails the alteration, invention and reinvention of traditions. Except in periods when there is a stress on the value of a break with the past, change is in large part acceptable to much of the population, precisely because it does not disrupt their sense of continuity too seriously. The impact of disrupting this by minor changes, such as altering coins and telephone kiosks, or by more sweeping social changes, such as the collapse of traditional shopping patterns and practices, or the enforced movement of people from condemned housing into modern projects that lack much of a sense of community, or large-scale immigration, can cause much anxiety and irritation, and can lead to a sense of loss of identity and community. This probably accounts for some of the Brexit vote in 2016, and is presented most clearly in unease about large-scale immigration, notably in areas where it is recent.

At the crucial level of change and related anxieties, the notion of European community is of value if its institutional pretensions and prerogatives do not range too widely, and are restricted by the preservation of a major role for the nation state. Telling people and their elected representatives that, as they are Europeans, they must act, indeed think, in a certain fashion is unacceptable in a democratic society. In defending the configuration and continuity of British practices, whether within or outside the EU, politicians are not fighting for selfish and foolish national interests but, instead, for the sense of the living past that is such a vital component of a people's understanding, acceptance and appreciation of their own society and identity.

NOTES

1. FROM THE IRON AGE TO THE REFORMATION

1. L. Jensen (ed.), *The Roots of Nationalism: National Identity Formation in Early Modern Europe, 1600–1815* (Amsterdam, 2016).

2. FROM THE REFORMATION TO THE GLORIOUS REVOLUTION, 1533–1688

1. J. Boys, *London's News Press and the Thirty Years War* (Woodbridge, 2011).

3. THE EIGHTEENTH CENTURY

1. J. Black, *Kings, Nobles and Commoners: States and Societies in Early Modern Europe—A Revisionist History* (London, 2004).
2. J. Black, 'Meeting Voltaire', *Yale University Library Gazette*, 66 (1992), pp. 168–9; R. Butterwick, *Poland's Last King and English Culture: Stanisław August Poniatowski 1732–1798* (Oxford, 1998).
3. G. Lesage, *Remarques sur l'Angleterre* (Amsterdam, 1715); Holbach, *Système social* (3 vols., London, 1774), II, 66–76; J. Lough, *The Encyclopédie* (London, 1971), pp. 297, 318–19.
4. Weichman, Brunswick representative at Hamburg, to Karl, 23 Nov. 1740, Wolfenbüttel, Staatsarchiv 1 Alt 22, 749 fol. 89.
5. *Craftsman*, 22 July 1732; *Fog's Weekly Journal*, 24 March, 21 April 1733.
6. BL, Add. 12130 fols. 53–5; W. Cobbett, *The Parliamentary History of England* (35 vols., London, 1806–20), IX, 1239, XI, 207.

7. R. Browning, *Political and Constitutional Ideas of the Court Whigs* (Baton Rouge, Louisiana, 1982).

8. J. Lockman, *A New History of England* (London, 1794 edn), pp. ix–x.

9. Trevor to Lord Grenville, Foreign Secretary, 8 Oct. 1792, NA. Foreign Office 67/10.

10. Cobbett, *Parliamentary History*, XI, 338.

11. J. Black, *Geographies of an Imperial Power: The British World, 1688–1815* (Bloomington, Indiana, 2018).

12. G. Plank, *Rebellion and Savagery: The Jacobite Rising of 1745 and the British Empire* (Philadelphia, 2006).

13. P. Taylor, *Indentured to Liberty: Peasant Life and the Hessian Military State, 1688–1815* (Ithaca, New York, 1994).

14. R. Szostak, *The Role of Transportation in the Industrial Revolution: A Comparison of England and France* (Montreal, 1991).

15. E.A. Wrigley, *The Path to Sustained Growth: England's Transition from an Organic Economy to an Industrial Revolution* (Cambridge, 2016).

16. J. Mokyr, *A Culture of Growth: The Origins of the Modern Economy* (Princeton, New Jersey, 2017).

17. L. Prados de la Escosura (ed.), *Exceptionalism and Industrialisation: Britain and Its European Rivals, 1688–1815* (Cambridge, 2004).

4. THE LONG NINETEENTH CENTURY

1. S. Heffer, *The Age of Decadence: Britain 1880 to 1914* (London, 2017).

2. T.G. Otte, '"Only Wants Quiet Riding"? Disraeli, the Fifteenth Earl of Derby and the "War-in-Sight" Crisis,' in G. Hicks (ed.), *Conservatism and British Foreign Policy, 1820–1920: The Derbys and Their World* (Farnham, 2011), pp. 103–6.

3. G. Hicks, 'An Overlooked Entente: Lord Malmesbury, Anglo-French Relations and the Conservatives' Recognition of the Second Empire, 1852,' *History*, 92 (2007), pp. 187–206 and *Peace, War and Party Politics: The Conservatives and Europe, 1846–1859* (Manchester, 2007).

4. J.P. Parry, 'Disraeli and England,' *Historical Journal*, 43 (2000), pp. 699–728.

5. Malmesbury circular, 8 Mar. 1858, NA. FO. 83/185, quoted in T.G. Otte, '"A Very Internecine Policy": Anglo-Russian Cold Wars before the Cold

War,' in C. Baxter, M.L. Dockrill and K. Hamilton (eds.), *Britain in Global Politics, vol. I: From Gladstone to Churchill* (Basingstoke, 2013), p. 24.

6. P. Nockles and V. Westbrook (eds.), *Reinventing the Reformation in the Nineteenth Century: A Cultural History*, special issue of the *Bulletin of the John Rylands Library*, 90 (2014).

7. M. Ković, *Disraeli and the Eastern Question* (Oxford, 2011).

5. THE TWENTIETH CENTURY

1. P. Dennis and J. Grey, *The Boer War: Army, Nation, and Empire* (Canberra, 2000).

2. P. Williamson, *Stanley Baldwin: Conservative Leadership and National Values* (Cambridge, 2007).

3. A. Roberts, *Eminent Churchillians* (London, 1994).

4. J. Stapleton, *Sir Arthur Bryant and National Identity in Twentieth Century Britain* (London, 2005).

5. A. Bosco, *June 1940, Great Britain and the First Attempt to Build a European Union* (Newcastle, 2016).

6. M. Ković, *Disraeli and the Eastern Question* (Oxford, 2011).

7. N. Ridley, *'My Style of Government': The Thatcher Years* (London, 1991), p. 159; Thatcher, 'The World at One', Radio 4, 20 Jan. 1993.

8. D. Heater, *The Idea of European Unity* (Leicester, 1992), pp. 152–3.

9. P. Ziegler, *Edward Heath* (London, 2010), pp. 107–8.

10. C.J. Bartlett, *British Foreign Policy in the Twentieth Century* (London, 1989), pp. 118–20.

11. A. Milward, *The Rise and Fall of a National Strategy, 1945–63* (London, 2002).

12. A. Hoare, *Macmillan, vol. II, 1957–1986* (London, 1989), pp. 328–9, 446.

13. R.F. Dewey, *British National Identity and Opposition to Membership of Europe, 1961–63: The Anti-Marketeers* (Manchester, 2009).

14. M. Haussler, 'The Popular Press and Ideas of Europe: The *Daily Mirror*, the *Daily Express*, and Britain's First Application to Join the EEC, 1961–63', *Twentieth Century British History*, 25 (2014), p. 121.

15. Anon., 'Public Opinion and the EEC', *Journal of Common Market Studies*, 6, 3 (1967–8).

16. Quoted in R. Gibson, *Best of Enemies: Anglo-French Relations since the Norman Conquest* (2nd edn, Exeter, 2004), pp. 288–9.

17. A. Spelling, 'Edward Heath and Anglo-American Relations 1970–1974: A Reappraisal', *Diplomacy and Statecraft*, 20 (2009), pp. 638–58; D.D. O'Hare, *Britain and the Process of European Integrity: Continuity and Policy Change from Attlee to Heath* (London, 2013).

18. L.J. Robins, *The Reluctant Party: Labour and the EEC* (Ormskirk, 1979).

19. R. Saunders, *Yes to Europe! The 1975 Referendum and Seventies Britain* (Cambridge, 2018).

20. I. Crewe and M. Harrop (eds.), *Political Communications: The General Election Campaign of 1983* (Cambridge, 1986) and *Political Communications: The General Election Campaign of 1987* (Cambridge, 1989).

21. D. Healey, *The Time of My Life* (1989; 1990 edn), pp. 458–9.

22. G. Bennett, *Six Moments of Crisis: Inside British Foreign Policy* (Oxford, 2013), p. 154.

23. A. Gamble, 'Europe and America', in B. Jackson and R. Saunders (eds.), *Making Thatcher's Britain* (Cambridge, 2012), p. 232. For the contrasting approaches of Thatcher and Blair to America, J. O'Sullivan, 'Serving to Win', *New Criterion*, 32, 5 (Jan. 2014), pp. 16–22.

24. *Spectator*, 12 July 1990.

25. F. Bozo, *Mitterrand, the End of the Cold War, and German Unification* (New York, 2009); Hurd, contribution to the 'Tory World' conference, University of Exeter, 20 June 2013.

26. D. Baker, A. Gamble and S. Ludlam, 'The Parliamentary Siege of Maastricht 1993: Conservative Divisions and British Ratification', *Parliamentary Affairs*, 47 (1994), pp. 37–60.

27. Sir Richard Body resigned the whip of his own volition in order to join the others, making the 'whipless nine'.

28. I. McAllister and D. Studlar, 'Conservative Euroscepticism and the Referendum Party in the 1997 British General Election', *Party Politics*, 6 (2000), pp. 359–71.

29. A. Bland, 'The Baby Sitter', *The Independent Magazine*, 9 Nov. 2013, p. 14.
30. B. Cash, 'Rotten Parchment Bonds,' *European Journal*, 12, 2 (Feb. 2005), p. 2.

6. BRITAIN AND EUROPE TODAY

1. D. Cameron, 'Free Movement within Europe Needs to Be Less Free', *Financial Times*, 27 Nov. 2013.
2. *Sunday Times*, 22 Dec. 2013.
3. A. Seldon and P. Snowden, *Cameron at 10: The Verdict* (London, 2016), p. 558.
4. M. Mosbacher and O. Wiseman, *Brexit Revolt: How the UK Left the EU* (London, 2016), p. 121; P. Manent, 'Les Gouvernants ne nous représentent plus, ils nous surveillent', *Le Figaro*, 1 August 2016, p. 19.

INDEX

INDEX

INDEX

INDEX

INDEX

INDEX

INDEX

INDEX

INDEX

INDEX

INDEX

INDEX

INDEX

INDEX

INDEX

INDEX

INDEX

Latin, 5, 19, 104

Latvia, 138

Laud, William, 31

Lawrence, David Herbert, 107, 118

Lawson, Nigel, 172

Lee, William, 51–2

Leeds Mercury, 60

Leeds, 191

legal system, 20, 43, 67, 69, 72
    common law, 2, 20, 37, 43, 61
    property, 57, 72

Leicester Square, London, 95

Leipzig, 107

Leo XIII, Pope, 112

Leopardi, Giacomo, 104

Leopold I, King of the Belgians, 100

Lesage, Georges-Louis, 53

lettres de cachet, 62

Liberal Democrats, 186, 187, 191

Liberal Party, 98, 114, 127

Liberal Unionists, 126

liberalism, 101, 103, 106, 107, 116, 117–19

liberty, 6, 52, 58–61, 63, 95, 111–12, 129, 183

Libya, 193

Licensing Act (1695), 51

Lichtenberg, Georg Christoph, 54

Life and Times of Stein, The (Seeley), 113

Life of Jesus, The (Strauss), 119

Life of Schiller (Carlyle), 118

Lincoln, 18

linguistic nationalism, 53–4

Lisbon, 16, 101

Liszt, Franz, 106

literature, 19, 20, 55, 66–8, 104, 107, 109–10, 117, 128, 131–2, 138

Lithuania, 138

'little Britains', 135

Little Dorrit (Dickens), 104

Little Ice Age, 41

Liverpool, Lord, *see* Jenkinson, Robert

Lloyd, Selwyn, 144

Lockman, John, 61

Lollard movement (c. 1382–1527), 14, 31

London, 37, 42, 93, 95, 136
    Amsterdam, relations with, 42, 56
    and Brexit, 190, 192
    finance, 99
    Franco-British Exhibition (1908), 125
    Georgian period (1714–1837), 52–3, 54, 55, 56, 64, 65
    Gordon Riots (1780), 76
    Great Exhibition (1851), 95
    Haynau's visit (1850), 108–9
    independence, 192
    Medieval period (c. 600–1485), 25
    newspapers, 52–3, 58
    polemic nationalism, 52–3
    policing, 120
    Reformation (c. 1527–58), 31

238

INDEX

INDEX

INDEX

INDEX

INDEX

INDEX

INDEX

INDEX

INDEX

INDEX

INDEX

INDEX

INDEX

INDEX